Emergence

Emergence

A Journey to New Beginnings

Nancy Sailer

RESOURCE *Publications* • Eugene, Oregon

EMERGENCE
A Journey to New Beginnings

Resource Publications
An Imprint of Wipf and Stock Publishers
199 W. 8th Ave., Suite 3
Eugene, OR 97401

www.wipfandstock.com

PAPERBACK ISBN: 978-1-6667-1231-5
HARDCOVER ISBN: 978-1-6667-1232-2
EBOOK ISBN: 978-1-6667-1233-9

07/14/21

Contents

Preface

I GREW UP IN a small town, longing for life in a fast-paced city filled with endless opportunities. I gazed into the clouds and dreamed of amazing, far-away places. I heard an airplane humming faintly in the distance and imagined it taking me to a thrilling, new life. I envisioned myself as a frequent traveler—full of knowledge and experience—an authentic world-changer.

I spent years studying and preparing, and worked desperately toward independence to make my dream a reality. I had no inhibitions and sprinted toward the finish line. What I did not realize was that the "magical place" would render me completely vulnerable and exposed.

As time went by, circumstances morphed my life into something almost unrecognizable. My journey had become laced with experiences that I could hardly believe were my own. How had everything become so twisted? Each decision skewed my path further from the safety that I had originally viewed. The world had proven cruel and sucked me in. My expectations were far from my dreamy vision.

I recalled the hum of that tiny airplane I had peeked at years before—so high in the sky—until the memory became faint. Then there was only silence.

I had carried misconceptions that propelled me into desperate situations, all the while fighting a battle for any meaningful step. But the more I fought, even with the purest intentions, the more snared and intertwined I became. It was futile.

I realized that although I had assumed a beginning without burdens—and had run intentionally and energetically toward my perfect plan—my baggage had become exceedingly heavier with each passing year. I could not shake it. The weight began to crush every step, causing destruction the second I attempted any new choice.

I pressed onward only to get caught in a brutal tailspin that played on constant loop. It seemed impossible to escape. I could feel a force pulling close by, barely out of my grasp. I knew it would lead to my rescue. If only I could get close enough.

I struggled to close the gap. In exasperation I realized I could never complete the bridge. When I felt I was positioned with the correct tools, I was missing the materials. When I had the materials, the tools seemed to disappear. The timing was never right. Circumstances kept misaligning and pushed me into the realization that I could no longer rely on my own abilities.

Surely there was an alternate universe that I had completely missed. How had so many years gone by and success seemed no closer than when I started? I was riddled with old wounds haphazardly stitched together that left jagged scars.

I had spent years chiseling my perception of people, circumstances, and the world. But it only had the resemblance of a hardened blob. It lacked shape and recognition and certainly was no work of art, although the effort that had gone into creating it was exhausting. I had continuously chipped away, convinced I would develop a masterpiece, only to produce an unrecognizable form.

The longer I rode the whirlwind, my expectations changed from exceptional to ordinary, then eventually to merely tolerable. If I could just slow the chaos, or disengage from the entanglement, I could still find a way out. I needed to catch my breath. I refused to lose the view that I could somehow fix it.

I thought endlessly about my many missteps in hopes of finding a different outcome. I came across an occasional high where I felt the possibilities from a fresh angle, only to crash into the reality that it was temporary. Nothing could sustain me. I longed for solid ground without peaks and valleys. But instead, I walked in a truth that led to self-blaming and the affirmation of my lack of abilities.

Out of desperation, I ventured into a new place willing to take one more step. I was tattered, broken, and empty when I entered into a covenant with the One that saved my life.

I became curious about the possibility of an authentic and sturdy foundation and a new form of stability. I began reading and studying to answer questions and increase my understanding of his divinity and power. I had the elementary view that as I learned, I would gain knowledge. However, I ultimately came to realize that as I grew in faith, it promoted wisdom. I was in a committed relationship with someone who loved me regardless of my bumps, bruises, scars, misperceptions, and flat-out terrible decisions.

For the first time in my life, I did not feel misunderstood, trapped, and exhausted. For once, I was capable and powerful and had much to offer. The bridge was finally built, and I was standing in the center confidently without concern of its collapse. I had assurance it would not only hold me but link my riddled past to a future filled with promises I had searched for.

I knew I wanted the Creator of the universe to be the one I recognized for bringing breath into my lungs. To be my ultimate voice of reason. And to be the one who counseled me through difficult situations.

An *emergence* had taken place. The birth of someone that had been there all along. I had felt suppressed, afraid, and ultimately been blinded to the abilities that were present. But once things came into focus, the burdens fell away, and my steps became lighter. I had always been capable, but my feelings had led me to believe otherwise.

I realized the source of my power and was beginning to understand the faith I needed to take steps. I came to know the ability of feeling energized, even when the cards were not stacked in my favor. Also, that there is no such thing as luck, but a greater force overseeing my daily decisions. I came to count on protection from the One that I surrendered to daily.

By spending time in a more attentive posture, I was not lacking in any area. Even if what surrounded me did not logically appear to be enough, my faith was a testament to the new meaning of the word. What developed was a realization that the world's offerings would never be sufficient. Not from my past, in the present, or for the future.

Once I peered into this untapped view, everything took on a different form. All things seemed possible, even if not necessarily easier. People were more important, even if often unlovely and disappointing. There was an existing purpose, even if I was not yet aware of the full extent of the steps. The idea that I could see things clearly became evident through the lens of the Word. I was motivated to saturate myself with truth. I was part of a masterpiece.

As my internal flame grew, it illuminated more possibilities. Distractions and missteps happened less frequently. And forward propulsion was more evident. Although I still strayed from the manicured path, I was no longer entrapped and rendered ineffective.

My increased study brought with it the wisdom that I had already possessed these qualities. But layers of distraction had skewed my steps from where they should have been. For years I felt as though I had attempted to travel a long journey on an empty tank, sputtering along with a dying engine. But once filled, I could navigate the journey without the fear of missing my destination. And most importantly, I knew it was real.

Acknowledgments

I FIRST WANT TO thank God who has made this journey possible. Without him, there would be no hopeful story, truthful information, or light to spread. Thank you for giving me the wisdom to share your truths and desires. I pray I have accomplished what you intended.

I would also like to thank Bryan, my incredible husband and teammate for life; for your endless support, encouragement, and time sacrificed. Thank you for inspiring me to continue writing.

Thank you to my amazing girls who are so unique in individual ways. I am appreciative for all that you teach me and how you constantly nudge me into more growth. Thank you for your willingness to share me with so many other young ladies who have captured my heart over the years.

Introduction

Over time, it has become evident that emergence is a true concept. It has been studied from both scientific and personal views. For the sake of comprehension, there are a few examples we will begin with that can enhance the perception of emergence. Although overall, our focus will be on the idea of emergence of our human spirit. The being that God placed within us. God has shaped our spirits to guide us and embrace the purpose we were placed on the Earth to accomplish.

The first example of emergence involves a seed that is concealed below the ground, not yet visible above the top layer of soil. Seeds in their primary stage need to germinate. They require the right conditions to take root and sprout. As a seed grows, it uses nourishment from the soil and transitions from one stage to another. This enables the seed to move from a state of darkness into light. As it emerges from the ground, the seed continues the journey to maturity.

Emergence is also displayed when entities persistently bring change. An illustration of this is an area of undeveloped land growing into a major metropolitan city. Over time, the skyline is altered and the territory that was once flat land becomes a thriving city, a continuous development of new structures that were not evident before. Perseverance made the city a possibility.

The final representation of emergence is the idea of numerous parts working together to create a whole. A system which requires the use of all portions to function for one intention. In this description, we imagine the human body. Cells work cohesively and create organs, which then work toward a certain purpose and in a specific manner. Think of a heart. In its intricacy, it has over a billion cardiac muscle cells. A portion of these cells do not create the heart's pumping motion. But operating together, they allow it to pump flawlessly for years to come.

The commonality in each example is function through unity. The seed is reliant on the soil. The landscape is altered by people working together. And the cells in sync bring forth the purpose for which they were designed.

In addition, all have steps that take place in order. None show a completed form that occurs immediately. Growth not only takes nurturing, but it takes time. The seed requires the right conditions to emerge from the ground. The city is built with perseverance, but over time. And the body is developed and formed in a mother's womb prior to the full display of its functionality.

The intention of gaining knowledge, even minimal understanding, is not designed to be a fast track. With time spent growing and learning, more areas develop than just our comprehension. Our character also increases. In essence, the gains encompass a more complete part of us. Not only our minds or hearts. They are reflected in our human spirit.

The overall view of emergence was initiated during the creation with God's involvement in the development of all things. When this concept is considered, we begin to understand that all aspects of emergence have one original foundation: our Creator, God the Father. This includes us and each characteristic that we possess, which emerge under proper conditions.

When considering emergence in our own lives, we should rely on God to be our daily partner. There are steps to be taken for learning and growth. Full fruitfulness does not happen immediately as our worldly perspective prefers. But with the right nourishment, we transition from darkness to light.

The Bible makes it clear that when we surrender to God—and accept the salvation he has offered us through Jesus—we have been prepared for the reception. The Spirit of God becomes one with our human spirit. In truth, our spirit longs to join with his.

This is seen in John 3:6 when speaking of being born again, born of the Spirit. This teaches that God had already prepared his place within us. To fulfill his desire for salvation, protection, and guidance, we simply need to accept him.

It is also referred to in Romans 8:16. "The Spirit Himself testifies with our spirit that we are God's children." This creates the view that the Spirit of God helps us realize we are heirs to his throne. We are seated as princes and princesses—dearly loved.

Finally, John 4:24 explains how we are aligned to worship. "God is spirit, and his worshipers must worship in the Spirit and in truth." This shows that our human spirits have been primed with the desire to join God in a way that no other part of our minds or hearts can. With complete commitment.

These passages teach that although our spirits may be muted, distracted, buried, and overrun by the world, God is able to clearly communicate with us. He can assist in the emergence of our true identities. We only need to be willing.

Just as there is a God who formed us in our mother's womb—and planned to exist within our spirit—there is an enemy who strives to keep us rendered ineffective. He wreaks havoc on our souls—thoughts and emotions—and bodies. We will review multiple areas of offense that the devil uses in attempt to keep us misguided. He operates in any capacity to discourage us from experiencing the rewards that God intended.

During this journey, we will address actions, characteristics, and emotions. We will learn of action steps that must be taken—although the taunting of the world claims they are impossible to achieve. Emotions can dismantle our peace; even the same, difficult emotions multiple times over. Occasionally we identify the characteristics that develop from emotions, but do not always understand how they directly correlate. It takes discipline and revelation, but it can be accomplished.

This book has a total of twenty-six chapters. Each is designed for teaching and review. They are intended to be pondered and used for enlightenment and in turn spiritual growth. Since the information is designed to be absorbed, it is suggested that one chapter be studied—either daily or weekly—depending on the pace of desired achievement. Any area that encourages the mind or convicts the heart should be savored and magnified for reflection. These are topics which will prove most beneficial. In addition, continued review will promote further understanding as various seasons of life are experienced.

Suggested reading:

The numbers twenty-six and fourteen represent salvation and rescue. Fourteen also symbolizes a double portion of power and completion; God's spiritual perfection.

Weekly: Twenty-six chapters reviewed twice yearly.

Daily: One chapter each day. (Fourteen opportunities for completion during a year).

If you believe you were destined for something greater—but are convinced you have missed opportunities—this is your time to shine. If you feel exhausted, shameful, lost, or lonely, come along on this journey of emergence. Learn how new beginnings can become your reality.

Action Steps

Now that you know these things,
you will be blessed if you do them.

JOHN 13:17

Perspective

THE IDEA OF PERSPECTIVE is perhaps one of the most vital. Choosing a correct frame of mind can uplift spirits and unveil possibilities in what seems impractical. It can encourage increased faith, bring forth power, and birth many important foundational concepts.

In its most basic form, perspective can be described as the way in which we see things. Possessing a negative or down-turning viewpoint delivers difficulty, and often brings mental or emotional burden. It can encourage incorrect steps and single handedly smother purpose. An inappropriate perception can kill potential before an initial thought is ever formed.

On the contrary, a positive perspective brings forth hope, possibility, encouragement, joy and even curiosity. When we operate in a realm of correct outlooks, new prospects appear. We become more comfortable with unfamiliar portions of our life because we hold the mindset that we are protected and powerful.

In his Word, God teaches that we were made in his image. Genesis 1:26 shapes the idea of our importance to him. It portrays that nothing can take the place of the endearing and all-encompassing love he has for us. God does not focus on what we have done and who we have been, but rather on what we are doing and who we are becoming.

In addition to being made in his image, Genesis 5:1 describes how we are made in his likeness. Image is how God placed his Spirit in us. And we realize that we are his children. The heirs to his throne. However, the idea of God's likeness models the value of our character. This concept is delivered by our choices; those things that are part of our free will.

God desires us to understand that we are made in his image. And that through correct perspective, we can obtain a life in which we operate in his likeness; making determinations which are pleasing to him, and that build our faith. However, skewed views pull us in the opposite direction toward a worldly frame of mind of self and others. This promotes difficulties in relationships and situations. It challenges our resemblance of God and tempts us down a more grueling path.

We often have an incorrect foundational outlook of God. We have readily taken on the belief that good works and correct actions are what please him. We learn by input from others, situations, or ill-advised decisions. We assume that only when we determine the correct or perfect path does he love or bless us.

Nothing could be further from the truth. This mindset disrupts progression. God wants us to realize that we are dearly loved because we are his, already appointed. No matter what mistakes we have made or will make. He loves us and will always be with us.

Our Father does not expect discovery of his likeness through solitude, but rather by remaining close to him. Religion, choices, or carefully planned steps do not supersede the relationship God desires. A simplistic realization. But our logic too often ushers in beliefs that leave us feeling lost, defeated, and unloved.

Our view of God's perfection brings forth judgment and comparison of ourselves and others, too often magnifying the belief that we should somehow be comparable to his greatness and divinity. But God never meant for that to be the case. Only through him are we righteous and whole. Not by our own power, wisdom, or abilities.

His Word also teaches of our fallen world. And that only the blood and resurrection of Jesus bring us near to him. He knows we are not worthy. But because God desires a relationship, he made a way. Our Father erased our sins and provided a place with him. Forever. This is not a truth that pertains only when we get everything right and make correct choices. It is *always* so.

We forgo any thoughts that determine judgment of our ability to be near God. Beliefs that are reasons to stay distant. Or that we cannot remain in his presence. We replace these with his sincere truth. Although our Father is perfect, he has never expected us to be.

To bring forth a more continuous positive perspective, try embracing the truth that a plan was put in place long ago to free us from our shortcomings. That while God possesses unending power and divinity, we are his focus. He has an intended purpose, and is encouraging us to increase our likeness of him. So that we become motivated for our designed objective. When we feel other than dearly loved, we revel in the majesty that the One who made the universe favors us. God put breath in our lungs and chose us.

To learn these truths, we saturate ourselves with his Word, and let it permeate our hearts. We ask God daily to guide our clarity of Scripture to develop exactly what he needs. To stay motivated, so that we can have a sturdy foundation. As our spirits absorb this certainty, it brings us closer to our intended place. An authentic relationship in which our likeness of God emerges.

Hope

PART OF THE CHALLENGE we face in worldly situations is an absence of hope. Hope is a general idea that we have something to look forward to or an entity to grasp. Even that we anticipate a situation will happen. But there is a portion of hope that is often overlooked. Because of the emotions that frequently cloud this concept, we become discouraged and disappointed when we fail to see the desired outcome. When it is stated, "I won't get my hopes up," this has taken place.

Often when our thoughts transition from an optimistic state to one of lack, we base reactions on negative viewpoints. Our hope comes from the confidence that we place in our abilities or the people we depend on. But when this occurs, possibilities often begin to dwindle, until we reach the conclusion that we never should have adopted a positive posture at all. We are treading in a realm of hopelessness. At this point, we have difficulty believing the likelihood of anything productive.

Delving deeper, we see that hope can be addressed when exploring expectations. An expectation is a view based on our thoughts and what we figure will happen. Combining this with hope is not necessarily seeing a situation logically, but assuming it will take place. Perhaps even an event which we have never experienced, but one we desire. This hope is based on and measured by our longing: how much we want it.

With that in mind, we understand that the concept of hope is driven by our desires. But it is often based on our expectations.

It can disintegrate when we feel the lack of assumed progress. This type of hope is initiated from within. Its foundation stems from our thoughts. It quickly waivers depending on our circumstances.

God has invited us to an alternate hope. Authentic in him. From a Biblical stance, an increase in hope is accompanied with confidence in God's promises. His Word teaches us how to grow in these truths, which increases our faith.

This type of hope not only creates a closer relationship, but newfound confidence in the areas of our lives where we are faltering. The wavering mindset will cease. Increased hope through God works miracles in our perspective and encourages growth in our character.

This model cannot be gained from our thoughts, emotions, or guidelines. It is only achieved through belief that God is present in the situation. As the Word teaches in Proverbs 3:5, we cannot depend on our own understanding when walking in the ways of God. Our minds cannot comprehend all the possibilities. Much less understand the fulfillment experienced when we rely on his promises. Or his abilities versus our own.

Isaiah 40:31 sums this up best: "But those who hope in the Lord will renew their strength. They will soar on wings like eagles; they will run and not grow weary; they will walk and not be faint." This can only be attained by the power of our Father.

In summary, correct perspective is vital in gaining a hopeful stance. But too often we rely on our personal desires to guide this. However, when we turn to God in these situations, we will increase authentic hope and achieve much more than merely a logical outlook.

Faith

Have you ever heard the phrase "seeing is believing"? We count something as truth when it is tangible. We use this logic readily to reason through circumstances. It might be that we have seen an occurrence and assume it will continue in that same manner. We consider examples as evidence. We put trust in them. There is a reliability that comes with trust.

When building relationships with others, we desire certainty in them. There is a settled feeling that comes when we can count on others. And believe in situations surrounding them. We become reliant on trust and feel substantial because of it. The more reliable something is, the more trusting of it we grow.

Now consider faith. Faith is believing in that which we cannot see. Is it as effortless to find belief in what appears absent as in something you clearly see? For most of us, this is not the case. When we see it; we believe it. But otherwise comes the difficult task of convincing us.

Putting this into perspective, our mind naturally attempts to move into a realm that we feel is trustworthy and feeds our logic. A worldly view that brings forth comfort which we must experience to accept. The usual sentiments of doubt or disbelief are the course we take until an outlook can be proven.

When we believe in something—but not because we have observed it—we step into the concept of faith. Of course, this is more challenging than basing our confidence on what we see. But God is looking for those that are willing to take the leap. He needs us to trust him. To believe whole-heartedly that he recognizes us and will guide our steps.

When gaining a faith-filled perspective, we move in the area where our logic and abilities do not limit what we perceive. If we only walk out what we trust by sight, we will miss numerous amazing opportunities and encounters. But when we lean into the possibilities—because we believe in someone greater—it allows more faith in our situations. Our accomplishments will be much broader.

Remaining in a faithful relationship with God does have its challenges. We battle a worldly mindset. The temptation to veer toward dependence on what we see is overwhelming. It takes discipline to stay the course of faithfulness. God knows there is distraction when we are constantly bombarded by things of this world. He desires for us to celebrate our blessings—which takes faith—especially when what we see does not align.

How often in our daily walk do we expect the best, but what we receive has lesser result? Our minds attempt to convince with reasoning that we are not favored in our circumstances. Even the smallest disappointment can cause a breach in our faith.

When we view things from a logical perspective, we have stepped from a place of faith and are treading in a partial stance. A worldly view. Sometimes rather than stepping *from* faith, we have not yet truly experienced faith at all.

Imagine being tasked with spending an entire day standing only on one leg without allowing the other to touch the ground. Wobbly, unsteady, and off-balance. We would grow exhausted and feel like giving up. This is how partial faith feels. Instead, we have ability to stand strongly on a firm foundation by putting our weight, belief, and faith fully in God.

The Bible tells us to "walk by faith, not by sight" (2 Cor 5:7). However, it is difficult when we feel under attack. True faith maintains the mindset that situations taking place around us are only distractions from the greater view into eternity. One of the largest misconceptions we walk out is believing what we see and using that to guide our steps. Instead, forward propulsion can be accomplished by exploring an increased faith and more time with God. He will lead us in the right direction. "Things which are seen are temporary, but the things which are not seen are eternal" (2 Cor 4:18).

To build faith and a relationship with God, spend time worshipping him, stay in his Word, and pray for hunger and motivation to do both. God will honor our steps and recognize the efforts we make. He will magnify those things for us which are eternal. And help us overcome the worldly intrusions. His Word is like a compass that always leads us back to truth. It is the best way to guide our faith. "So then faith comes by hearing, and hearing by the word of God" (Rom 10:17).

It can be stated that hope is the belief that something *can* happen, but genuine, spirit-filled faith is the belief that it actually *will*. Believing and having faith toward the unseen increases our hope. True faith expands our belief that God is who he says he is and that his Word reigns true.

Surrender

THERE ARE MANY STEPS we take daily to fulfill responsibilities. Or simply to complete tasks that must be accomplished. Depending on organization, there may be schedules and plans laid out for a day, week, month, or even a year. But how often do best laid plans go awry? And kinks and unforeseen issues get thrown into the mix. These instances are often where stress is formed.

In addition, when considering our relationships, the thought of varying from our desired specifics makes us uncomfortable. We feel out of control. Naturally, we prefer to make our own decisions and maintain authority. Or at least operate under the idea that we realize the plan and what to expect.

These thoughts are represented by deciding the parameters of our steps. Our logical minds are more comfortable with the sensation of staying in control. As we reflect on our day, we enjoy the feeling that we chose steps which aligned correctly. We gain satisfaction from this mindset. Here we will examine a different perspective. A surrendered posture.

The word "surrender" often brings discomfort because it relates to a sensation of giving in, which means losing our ability to be right or stay in control. This is the outlook we have learned from our experiences and daily examples.

Regarding the heavenly realm, we will address submission and surrender. These two words are often used in conjunction when considering the topic of faith. Or sometimes are even interchanged. Here we will specify the difference between the two.

Submission is the act of *yielding* to a higher force or authority. Surrender is to *stop resisting* and then submit to authority. If viewed in this way, the act of submission is a part of surrendering. We can submit without surrendering. But are unable to fully surrender without submitting.

To increase our faith and have a true relationship with God, we surrender to him and commit our lives to fulfilling what he has planned. The first step in this act of surrender is to stop fighting what God wants to do in our lives. We cannot lead while he is leading.

We submit our hearts, minds, and spirits to the truth that he dearly loves us and knows our needs beyond our capacity. We stop making excuses as to why circumstances may not be good for us, or why we do not want to carry out certain situations.

This mindset displays that we can give more of ourselves to God because he is trustworthy. This act of submission leads to a place of comfort with a less resistive posture. However, a common problem is reasoning and consideration of what we might miss. But there is no need for concern. God always has better in store for us than we could ever plan.

Surrender should be viewed as the act of breaking down the parts that bring resistance to a relationship with God. This allows less of us and more of him. An absence of what is causing our distractions. And a filling of what needs to encompass our spirit.

We face challenges with this viewpoint because it is opposite our normal intention to maintain control. We strive daily to gain experience, increase our abilities, and for success with life in general. To concede anything seems unnatural. But it helps build a solid foundation in our journey with God.

When we stay fully surrendered, we do not feel hijacked by events of the day or other situations. In addition, exhaustion and frustration fall away. We feel confident that we are placed in the hands of the One that perceives what each day holds.

Imagine a tall maze and how much fun children have running full speed throughout. Without regard to misdirection or fear of choosing an incorrect path. They are confident they *will* locate the way out. They might take multiple wrong turns but are smiling and laughing the entire time. They have discovered joy in the journey.

Adults walk the same maze with a slower and more calculated approach. Depending on our perceptions, we may have feelings of isolation or fear. There is contemplation of where we have been, and where we need to go next. We take on a self-reliant attitude and mentally decipher the solution of how to get out. Even though we cannot view the other side, and everything looks the same. Adults are cautious and thoughtful within our own abilities. And might even become annoyed if it takes too long to locate the way.

In life, our daily walk is often represented by a similar mindset. We prefer to have questions answered before taking steps. Because we desire to stay in control, God often has difficulty reaching us. But our Father calls us to a childlike faith. In a similar manner to the kids in the maze who have confidence in *what* will happen. Not necessarily *how* it will take place. He wants us to relinquish control and retain the belief that while we only see the area in front of us, he has sight of the entire maze. God easily guides us where we need to go.

We only trust God to do this when we know who we are. In addition to whose we are. Made in his image and dearly loved. After all, we do not choose to walk with strangers but those we know.

A well-known verse in Scripture is Jeremiah 29:11. It states: "'For I know the plans I have for you,' declares the Lord, 'plans to prosper you and not to harm you, plans to give you hope and a future.'" However, people often stop without focus on verses twelve and thirteen which read: "'Then you will call on me and come and pray to me, and I will listen to you. You will seek me and find me when you seek me with *all* your heart.'"

This is true surrender. It shows God's promise and teaches us guidelines to what our steps are in the process. We have a responsibility. We are asked to seek him with our entire heart. Believing that we are whole and capable—only through him—allows us to trust that his words are true. "Those who leave everything in God's hand will eventually see God's hand in everything" (Unknown).

John 6:35 tells us, "I am the bread of life. Whoever comes to me will never go hungry, and whoever believes in me will never be thirsty." God is our daily bread. He brings nourishment and fulfillment. Although he never promised it would be easy, he has the answers. He perceives the way each day.

Our new views and increased faith allow a softening of the desire to maintain control and begin to alter our perspective of God taking the reins. We can relinquish ourselves to him. Although sometimes uncomfortable, with a continued decrease of resistance—and increase of submission—it becomes easier. More natural. Surrender is a daily decision that will change our lives.

Obedience

OBEDIENCE IS ANOTHER CONCEPT that often brings discomfort. We equate it with being told what to do. Whether we like it or not. This is often coupled with the concern of losing our control, as previously mentioned.

Obedience can be considered as a next step following surrender. In a cultural realm, it may take the form of receiving orders from our authority. Such as a boss, our parent, or a variety of leaders. In this view, obedience can encompass involvement with people whose abilities or knowledge may be questionable. Or someone we have concerns about. Even so, there are expectations for maintaining compliance.

In the spiritual realm, we show obedience to God. He has unmatched abilities and knowledge. So why is there often a lack of obedience regarding our focus on him?

The culprit is partial or absent faith. It might be the case that we are unsure we can trust and believe him. Or wonder if it is necessary to walk in obedience of someone we cannot see. Sometimes it even seems difficult to know what God is asking of us. We may try to guess or assume we have figured out his requests, but this can lead us down incorrect paths. And we would be amiss based on our speculation. It is easy to get caught up in "hearing" God in those things we want, or even walking confidently as though he has requested certain steps from us.

The only way to truly realize how God is directing our progression—and to stay obedient—is to remain close to him. He speaks quietly and asks us to draw near. We must do so to hear his words. An authentic relationship with time spent in worship, the Word, and prayer is the way to determine what is being requested.

Remember, our spirit joins with his when we worship. And we draw closer to him. In addition, God's Word allows us better insight into who he is. Finally, time in prayer—or conversation—teaches us what he desires and encourages a direct relationship. This can be simple dialogue, just as you would speak to a friend.

But this is challenging. Many grew up thinking, or still believe, that God is distant and inaccessible. A stern dictator that will scold us at the slightest misstep. However, 1 John 4:16 tell us, "God is love."

So why does the Bible tell us to fear God? Often this portrays the wrong impression and repels instead of drawing us closer to him. Let's look at this with the correct perspective to lay more groundwork for obedience.

Consider Proverbs 9:10: "The fear of the Lord is the beginning of wisdom, and the knowledge of the Holy One is insight." Think about the fear of the Lord simply as the desire to follow his Scripture or stay disciplined to it. Then ponder the verse under the premise that if we study what the Lord speaks, we will gain wisdom from him. And more insight into discovery of what he has for us. This will allow growth in relationship with God. And it will simultaneously encourage more obedience. Doors will open for increased communication to learn what he is asking of us.

This point is also brought to light in Psalm 25:12. It tells us that the person who fears the Lord will be shown by him what path to take. And will gain prosperity and inheritance from God. It will allow access to his great riches, the very blessings that God has ordained us to receive. Instead of casting a negative light on fear of God, we take the perspective that it is a healthy discipline that brings favor.

In addition, it is important to mention that a lack of obedience brings misstep. This can lead to gaps in our wholeness and often temptations toward a sinful nature. We have ability to remain in God's will, which we do by obedient steps. But instead, we often decide to venture out on our own. Remaining in God's will grants blessings and fruit. But the enemy has more room to work when we are operating of our own accord. Without guidance from God, there are increased opportunities for us to stumble.

Romans 12 tells us the following: "Therefore, I urge you, brothers and sisters, in view of God's mercy . . . do not conform to the pattern of this world but be transformed by the renewing of your mind. Then you will be able to test and approve what God's Will is—His good, pleasing and perfect Will" (vv. 1–2).

This again shows that by being disciplined to what God wants—and staying surrendered and obedient—we follow his path. If we keep our minds on the goodness of God daily, he gives us wisdom. We will be able to realize, without hesitation, what is pleasing to him. Instead of existing in a worldy realm surrounded by distractions.

Once we grow in relationship—and walk in more obedience—we hear God's voice magnified in our daily lives. He speaks in many ways: including dreams; whispers; through music; by things we read; and even by way of other people that speak into our lives. As our confidence grows by knowing God and discovering his will, we discern more easily what he is saying. Then obedience is no longer a chore, but rather a desire. "Whether you turn to the right or to the left, your ears will hear a voice behind you saying, 'This is the way; walk in it'" (Isa 30:21).

Forgiveness

THE GREATEST GIFT GOD has given us is the act of forgiveness. Jesus took the wrath that was meant for us by way of the cross. He became our sin so that we would not suffer the consequences that were due. And throughout the punishment, he was innocent. Our Father protected us and canceled the debt that we were in line to pay, so that we could walk in a new place called forgiven.

Just as we have choices and free will, so did Jesus. He was able to choose to walk out the penalty that set us free. In the garden, as Jesus prayed to God the Father for strength, he said, "Not my will but yours be done" (Mark 14:36). Although in agony and seeking a different way, Jesus walked out the will of his Father. His act was an amazing model of forgiveness in which he *chose* to take part.

How often do we seek the opportunity to decide a more lenient path for someone? Instead of selecting an alternate, harsh outcome? It is difficult for us to forgive those that offend. Even though Jesus modeled an endurance of persecution and torment, which promoted an alternate opportunity.

While living in this fallen world, we frequently encounter others who cause us pain or distress. And too often we refuse to show them the same forgiveness that Jesus displayed. Although he was totally innocent—and extended mercy—where we should have been responsible. We readily judge that others are undeserving of our forgiveness. However, it is not our position to decide who is worthy of pardon. Instead, we are called to absolve each person from what they have done to harm us.

God never expected us to walk this out alone. He is present when we need assistance bringing forgiveness to completion. Mercy of others is necessary because it frees us from remaining a prisoner. Unforgiveness steals our joy and keeps us in darkness, which causes us to veer from the likeness of God.

Bitterness also forms when we fail to forgive those that have hurt us. It can grow like a thorny bush with bristles and chokes out signs of life. It takes root and begins to spread to every part of our being, destroying us from the inside out. Until we dismantle this bitterness once and for all, we cannot walk in true freedom.

The harm someone has caused is a weight that we justify the need to continue carrying. It seems absurd to reason through why we should withhold forgiveness and allow it to drive spikes into us over and over. This takes place because we do not excuse actions when we deem the offense unacceptable.

But we are called to "be kind and compassionate to one another, forgiving each other, just as in Christ God forgave you" (Eph 4:32). This is easier said than done unless we trust God to assist us in walking it out. He never asked that we declare their actions tolerable. He wants us to forgive their transgression. This step does not reflect that they are right—but instead that Jesus is right.

When Jesus fulfilled forgiveness on the cross, he made a choice. We are asked to complete the act by extending pardon to those who surround us. Realizing we cannot change others—and accepting God's assistance—brings true absolution to the situation.

One additional aspect is unforgiveness of self. Perhaps there was a misstep, bad decision, or blame placed by our poor choices. Often this is one of the most difficult experiences to forgive because we cannot escape. But God will rescue us from the unsure footing of thoughts and emotions that accompany our own merciless cycles.

His love for us is greater than anything that may have taken place. It fights the idea that forgiveness is not deserved and cannot happen. Or perhaps we have attempted to take the step but continue to fall into a relentless rhythm of torment.

In this case, a new perspective is necessary. A belief that God no longer wants us to suffer from the situation. Remember, we were made in his image and hold a place near to his heart. He is available to guide us through forgiveness and into freedom from these burdens once and for all.

A great first step is drawing near to God in worship. When we relinquish our own thoughts to a posture of closeness, we begin to perceive things differently. He can administer clarity through this act. And when we choose to take the step, he meets us.

Next, we ask God to forgive us. When we repent, we have an honest heart and remorse for what took place. We also proclaim that we will turn from the act and the intent to repeat it. We allow God to move. Then praise him for forgiveness.

If we believe God and trust his process, we will be ushered into a new place with fresh incentive. One where we forgive those who have wronged us and can even forgive ourselves. We strip the enemy of his potential control, viewing us as a ridiculed sinner. And disallow the lie that we should keep our sin secret and walk shamefully. The devil's attempt is to convince us to remain trapped. Instead, we follow the steps God prepared and instructed. And we find freedom.

Gratitude

HAVE YOU HEARD IT said that we should "stop and smell the roses"? A phrase from Walter Hagen which expresses we should enjoy life and take time for observation. Or consider the quote by Melody Beattie that states, "Gratitude turns what we have into enough."

These thoughts bring forth the idea of thankfulness. In our world, it is easy to become enthralled with objects and desires. We often take note of what we seek more than take time to express appreciation. And our thanks are usually based on what we already have. Too frequently it takes sickness, death, or a traumatic experience for us to slow down and survey, or to perceive memories, highlights, and even possibilities.

The truth about gratitude is that we consider it the action of showing thanks for what we possess. This has even become the method of how we show honor to God. But there is more depth to gratitude than we often realize.

From gratitude emerges the correct, heart-felt posture that allows us to admit that there is someone more profound. He blesses us with amazing opportunities. It also affords us the accurate mindset that although we experience free will, God is in control of what we have. We could just as easily possess less. Or maybe we feel as though we are continuously shorted. Perhaps, it is difficult to honor God with thanksgiving. However, we should recall that all we own is not ours anyway.

In this context, we will remove judgment of God's reception of appreciation based on possessions, abilities, or health. Instead, we choose a disciplined action of recognition based on who he is. Considering how we were designed, and whose breath is in our lungs, encourages the image that we are highly favored by the One who created the world.

Perhaps if we stop placing specific guidelines on our gratitude, it will allow authentic acknowledgment. Especially since we were undeserving from the beginning. We are sinners that were escorted out of wrath and provided a way. Not through our own power, but by a sacrificial lamb.

Often, we thank others without a second thought. But we fail to make time—or take an opportunity—to thank the most important One. The statement we make so quickly and mindlessly to others is not as frequent for the Savior who granted our eternity. We should challenge ourselves to spend time daily in thanksgiving to God.

An additional concept is that gratitude is not simply showing thanks. With sincerity, it encompasses a posture that changes us from the inside out. Even if we assume there is nothing to be thankful for, we view gratitude in its most raw form. That we were chosen by someone who dearly loves us. "Give thanks to the Lord, for he is good; his love endures forever" (Ps 118:1).

Instead of following the mindset that "we have so we thank," perhaps we could revel in the reality that we are loved and have been granted everlasting life. A gift that everyone has received. And one we should be extremely appreciative for. This levels the playing field. It allows each of us to identify one incredible reason why we should display absolute gratitude and admiration of God each day.

The Bible speaks of honoring God and worshipping him with our words and through song. This sometimes causes an unsettled view. Worshipping has even acquired a negative connotation depending on our level of comfort. But in truth, we are creatures designed by God to join in spirit with him. When Scripture describes angels singing, we know that God loves music. We realize he made a way for us to draw near to him while expressing our gratitude.

Worship not only clearly displays love, appreciation, and admiration to our Creator, but it draws us closer to him in a peaceful and comforting manner. God's Word tells us that he inhabits our praise. It has been mentioned that gratitude changes us from the inside out. This is due to the intimacy we achieve with God.

Although this act of adoration is how we show our love to God—because he is an amazing Father—he created a benefit in it for us also. He has many qualities, and they begin to surface during our time of worship. In fact, God has many names. They are all advantageous to us: Creator; Strong Tower; Advocate; Wonderful Counselor; Prince of Peace; Purifier; Shepherd; the Almighty; Savior; Most High; God of Hope; Comforter; Redeemer; Shield; Healer; Messiah; and this is only a brief list. God has always planned to extend his benefits to us and can do so when we draw close in worship.

This not only gives us a different perspective of our surroundings, but it develops other characteristics that promote correct views. Specifically, of self and others. It softens our hearts. Worship invites clarity and affirmation to the path that God has planned. Gratitude allows us to receive and embrace what God desires for us. This supernaturally links us to our Father, with the reminder that we were made in his image and live in his likeness. That alone is worth all the gratitude we can express.

Power

True power cannot be discovered without discussing the Holy Spirit. As we unpack this, we will view multiple, diverse realms. His power can move mountains; increase hope; change hearts; and administer miracles. And no one is excluded.

As we walk through life remaining dependent only on our own abilities and strength, we miss the real concept of what God planned. We previously discussed the importance of staying surrendered and in his will. It is equally imperative when considering this concept.

First, let us look at the person of the Holy Spirit. The Trinity consists of God, Jesus, and the Holy Spirit. We have discussed our Father, and that we are made in his image and likeness. We have marveled at the sacrifice of Jesus, which allowed us forgiveness, freedom, and the ability to celebrate closeness. The third person is the Holy Spirit. He is vital and has many roles in our relationship with God.

As we live in this fallen world, we are naturally drawn to sin, thanks to the temptations and actions of the enemy. Earth is his playground. And he wants nothing more than to keep us in a vicious cycle. One that causes constant disruption in our lives. But the Holy Spirit begins his journey by drawing us in and impressing on us a desire to seek forgiveness. He allows us to see truth where it was not before evident. He ushers in the curiosity of an eternity with God. The Holy Spirit is our personal evangelist.

When we choose God as our Savior, the Holy Spirit is also extended the invitation and enters our lives. He possesses many abilities that encourage, improve, and guide us as we grow with God. As we ask for forgiveness of our sins, the Spirit sanctifies us, which purifies and sets us apart.

We cannot truly increase our likeness of God without the Holy Spirit. He acts only when he hears God's request and becomes a hope that grows our faith. But most importantly we learn that "no one can enter the kingdom of God unless they are born again" (John 3:3). This happens through the Holy Spirit. He renews our human spirits which have seen destruction by sin. Without him, we would not choose God or spend eternity in heaven.

God's Word tells us that his Spirit brings us knowledge. We are taught the promise that the Holy Spirit brings forth information we use to grow in the ways of our Lord. And that he picks up where Jesus left off on Earth. "All this I have spoken while still with you. But the Advocate, the Holy Spirit, whom the Father will send in my name, will teach you *all* things and will remind you of everything I have said to you" (John 14:25–26).

The Word explains that our power comes from the Holy Spirit. We begin to realize that he steers us to a place that allows God's strength to become our strength. In addition, we are taught that the Holy Spirit is powerful and all-knowing. Micah 3:8 tells us, "I am full of power by the Spirit of the Lord." In addition, we begin to discern the difference in worldly situations. And realize that we overcome because "the one who is in you is greater than the one who is in the world" (1 John 4:4).

Growing in clarity and closeness with God through the Holy Spirit convicts our hearts in many ways. Especially in wisdom of the Word. We realize that God gave the Holy Spirit authority to be a part of us and lead. We grow with God as we surrender and listen to the guidance of his Spirit. Our great Counselor.

Second Timothy 3:16–17 beautifully sums up the mighty power we possess by immersing ourselves in—and gaining revelation of—the Word. "*All* Scripture is God-breathed and is useful for teaching, rebuking, correcting, and training in righteousness, so that the servant of God may be thoroughly equipped for every good work."

This leaves no doubt that we are prepared for everything we face if we study God's truths. The "all" in this verse brings pause. It means *all* verses are useful. Not just our favorites. Or the ones we know by heart. There is something for every situation. Just as John chapter 14 tells us that the Holy Spirit will teach us *all*. This begs the question why we attempt to operate under our own power without consulting God's Spirit? Or before surrendering to his guidance in our steps?

The Word covers every part of our lives. And God gave us authority to use it. We are fully equipped and called to walk in this power. We should discipline ourselves to consult the Word—and the Holy Spirit—each day for decisions. Instead, we aimlessly step out on our own using logic that the world teaches. We forfeit the power that God intended. But the Holy Spirit can infuse us with knowledge, clarity, sanctification, and power. We will begin to experience what God has to offer on a whole new level.

Protection

As a continuation of the great power that we possess through the Holy Spirit, we will look at the protection afforded us by the Word of God. As was previously mentioned, the Word is God-breathed and pertinent to all situations that we encounter. There has always been a plan in place when it comes to guarding ourselves and those around us.

We saw how 2 Timothy displayed that the Spirit utilizes Scripture to increase our wisdom and shows us how to magnify the glory of God. Hebrews tells us, "The word of God is alive and active. Sharper than any double-edged sword, it penetrates even to dividing soul and spirit, joints and marrow; it judges the thoughts and attitudes of the heart" (Heb 4:12).

This powerful verse teaches how we were designed to use Scripture—not only as a spiritual compass, but also as a weapon. Understanding that God's words are "alive and active" brings forth mighty strength.

John 1:14 tells us, "The Word became flesh and dwelt among us." Hebrews 13:8 states, "Jesus Christ is the same yesterday, today and forever." We can surmise that God gifted us Jesus—his Living Word—to allow specific examples to grow our wisdom and to show us how to use his Word for protection. That has not changed. It never will. There is great comfort in its reliability, dependability, and eternal impact.

Jesus modeled for us in Matthew chapter 4 how to use Scripture to fight when he combatted the temptations of the devil in the desert. He was ordained to experience all that we face on Earth. Three times he quoted truths from Scripture as a guide to what we are capable of when partnered with the power of the Word. God showed him, and Jesus taught us. It required acceptance of what his Father had spoken and has now been written. It defeated the attempt at temptation.

This action is a great model for us as to the power that the Word holds. Recall how Satan was not deterred by Jesus or his identity. The devil still attempted to attack in his weakest moments. This exemplifies the constant action of our enemy. How much more will the devil try to coerce our lives if he had no fear of Jesus? The great news is that we have authority when using the Word as a weapon to defeat the devil. The Holy Spirit teaches us how to do this when we allow him to counsel.

Even greater is our protection from death—which was rendered ineffective—when Jesus conquered the cross. He could have fallen into temptation with Satan in the desert instead of saving us from our sins. But he chose us. His actions left a void for the devil. The enemy remains under our authority as we protect areas of our lives that he attempts to steal and destroy.

We must stay proactive. God granted us authority and expects us to use it for protection. It has already been issued and prepared. But too often we *wait* on God's response or for his actions. So how do we take the intended steps?

Just as a soldier does not leave his weapons behind when preparing for war, we should not be caught off-guard without ours. A warrior does not feverishly search for his battle gear just before he fights. Nor should we be distant from the word of God. Or keep it hidden until a time during which we feel the need to use it. Its truths should live in our hearts, be poised on our lips, and burst forth from our memories. We must saturate ourselves with it in preparation.

In addition, Ephesians chapter 6 teaches us about the Armor of God. Just as these pieces are utilized by an army for protection during war, so are we shown to use them in our everyday life. This is because we are under attack often by the enemy. We must not scurry to assemble when the time comes (v. 13). We should pray for covering daily in preparation for the schemes of the enemy.

Ephesians 6:14–17 shows us the pieces of armor. Surrounding the description, Paul gives an explanation that we are not at battle with those visibly around us, but to stay alert to the powers of the darkness in the spiritual realm. No distress is intended if there is not increased understanding of this. Ask the Holy Spirit to guide and bring forth wisdom of the steps for protection. He is ready and can easily do so if we are willing.

We will address each part of the Armor of God. Just as a belt goes around us in the natural, the belt in the spiritual armor keeps us surrounded by the word of God. And the truth referred to is Scripture. The breastplate of righteousness and the helmet of salvation protect our hearts and our minds from anything that might try to penetrate or distract our focus from God. The shoes of the gospel are used to readily spread the good word to others and teach about the peace that comes from knowing God.

The final two pieces are the shield of faith and the sword of the Spirit. These are not only for protection, but they are intended to be used offensively in battle. Scripture says that the shield "can extinguish all the flaming arrows of the evil one" (Eph 6:16). We keep it held high to disallow any schemes of the enemy. In addition, the sword of the Spirit is God's Word designed and intended for use—just as Jesus modeled—to combat the lies of Satan.

A powerful view to take is that we are ambassadors for God in this world. Prepared and equipped. And he relies on us to deliver his gospel. The enemy has a deep need to stop this from occurring. He will try to taint anything or hinder anyone that might be a threat to him. But we stand ready.

The word of God is sometimes described as old or ancient and not pertinent to our times. But when said, it becomes clear that the speaker has not yet learned of the mighty power the Word possesses. It is indeed our most effective weapon and spreads abundant hope. There is never a wrong time to press into the benefit of God's Word. Its truths can abolish any area where the devil tries to make a foothold. The enemy cannot render us ineffective.

Action Steps

It is the Holy Spirit's job to teach and instruct us. But it is our responsibility to seek and welcome his guidance and wisdom. Our willingness is important in this process and cannot be understated. It allows the Holy Spirit to lead us into full protection.

Healing

It is often expressed that time heals wounds. However, this is an incorrect notion. Time alone does not heal; it can generate more of a burden. Often memories get buried. But they have the tendency to surface when triggers take place. We cannot ignore or run from our situations, nor from ourselves. We are always there.

Whether immediate—or over time—instances in our lives cause a need for healing. Often, we view physical deficits as one of the most amplified. However, there are also circumstances that bring sought-after healing of the soul (thoughts and emotions). In fact, these are often complications that can continue—sometimes unidentified—as they steadily grow and become a part of us.

Culture recognizes that both physical and emotional needs are more rampant than ever and are unique for each of us. But often there is a spiritual component that goes unrecognized, even among believers. This can arise from a less-than-heightened comfort level concerning spiritual needs. But foundational guidelines can encourage correct focus, and healing can take place.

We will consider physical and mental healing as delivering freedom from injury or disease. And spiritual healing as rendering us sound or complete. There is importance in these viewpoints. The worldly definition of healing is bringing wellness to a recognized issue. But spiritual healing is assisting us to a place that increases our wholeness in God. And encourages a faithful mindset. Simply put, *an increase of God and a decrease of us.*

We first must recognize that spiritual imbalance is a real condition. Then, it is necessary to request the assistance of the Holy Spirit to identify any unsteady area. He will honor this. "Search me, God, and know my heart; test me and know my anxious thoughts. See if there is any offensive way in me, and lead me in the way everlasting" (Ps 139:23–24). As we identify any hinderances, we ask for forgiveness to bring us closer to God. And further down our path to "the way everlasting."

Absent of immediate influence from God, healing happens in stages. Science cannot reason through the unknown steps of God's will. It focuses on the tangible things of the world. There are names and parameters for ailments that society identifies. But too often, consideration is not given to the possibility of spiritual influence in worldly circumstances. Even more challenging, there is not a standard diagnostic tool that accompanies spiritual situations. It becomes our responsibility to seek deeper understanding and healing.

Just as we are encouraged to fulfill medical and emotional needs, we must be diligent to recognize what is lacking in our spirits. Careful and intentional care can encourage steps and bring protection from further deficiency. Many hindrances occur and become distractions to the completion we seek. Identification of these is imperative to keep from delaying our action steps.

The Word teaches us truths. The Holy Spirit assists with wisdom. And God often leads us through steps to grow our character and abilities. Things that are needed to fill our spirits which ultimately encourage steps toward wholeness. He ushers us into these stages and magnifies what is necessary to grow into a greater likeness of him.

An important step to true healing is correct perspective. We do not have answers as to why some are physically healed and others are not. We were never promised that God would grant this knowledge. He knows all but realizes that it is not necessarily advisable for us to gain the answers. Arriving at—and accepting—this conclusion helps us forgo the continued need to logically understand all things.

If we operate from a realm of insisted comprehension, we are expecting to possess the same infinite wisdom that God does. None of us are worthy of this. Nor do we have the capacity to contain it. Desperately chasing answers often leads to exactly the opposite of our desired outcomes.

The belief in God to make correct decisions is reflected in a quote by Philips Brooks: "Nothing lies beyond the reach of prayer except that which lies outside the will of God." This portrays that although we may pray desperately for our desired outcomes, if they are not in God's will, they cannot happen. Unfortunately, when attempting to make sense of things, we sometimes grow impatient or upset with God. However, an unexpected outcome should never render us silent from conversation with him.

When we pray for healing, we have specific focus on areas we deem necessities. Sometimes our situations appear more desperate. We may even feel trapped by our bodies or minds due to ailments or diseases. But too commonly, this invites perseveration on the very entities that are causing distraction from God.

While he invites us to pray and even petition, an incorrect focus encourages attention on the situation. Rather than the Healer. This allows a mimicked faith that may dwindle once a solution is delivered. Whether it aligns with our desired outcome or not.

Thoughts, problems, or even medical situations may seem to have no foreseen solutions. We focus desperately on our needs and lose sight of our whole beings. Are our spirits still getting fed? Are we walking close to God and listening to the Holy Spirit? And are we doing so for the right reasons? Or only for what we seek? These questions can assist in recognizing our spiritual condition.

While accepting the unknown—and facing less than desirable outcomes—we maintain the hope that God can and will bring healing. Only he has answers to our requests. We believe that our Father can deliver anything within his will. Guided by the Holy Spirit, we continue with steps toward our spiritual healing.

Stages to recognize God above our desires can be accomplished. We magnify reliance on him, listen to the Holy Spirit, and join with other believers. Unfortunately, this path is often overlooked. Instead, the focus is on more tangible situations that we readily experience in physical and emotional circumstances. Notions that may be seen more than believed, and assumed more than hoped for.

God has given an example of this faith in a story in Mark chapter 9. A doubtful father was asking for healing for his son. He inquired *if* Jesus could help. In verse twenty-three the father was told, "Everything is possible for one who believes." The boy's father cried out to Jesus to help him with his unbelief.

The father in this story had a desire of healing for his son. But there were periods of time when he thought there was no solution. Not in his logical assumption at least. This inspired his question to Jesus, which included *if*. The man was speaking to him, inquiring with a mind prepared for disappointment.

How often do we approach the Throne of God with a less-than-authentic belief? The fatigue of the world—along with our daily perceptions—can easily taint our zeal and boldness. What if God is looking for those that approach him with a hopeful belief in his true abilities?

The only way to gain complete healing from past circumstances—or present deficiencies—is to rely on the source that strengthens and sanctifies us. Our Savior. God the Father. With action steps guided by his Holy Spirit, we enter a realm in which we experience spiritual healing. Not based on remedies that the world defines. Instead, God's assurance and power will bring forth a magnification of his goodness. And will restore us from the inside out.

Commitment

It is often not challenging to stay committed when something matters greatly to us. This may include situations regarding children, a spouse, family, our jobs, money, time spent on specific hobbies, or even philanthropy. We can be committed to people or objects. However, we should not be blindly devoted to everything we deem as important.

When considering God's plan, we often find ourselves walking in areas we never should have encountered. We aimlessly, or even purposefully, step into circumstances not intended for us. But we have pledged our faith to them. Too frequently this takes place to please others or in an attempt to get ahead. But committed lives that position God first, truly surrendered, will allow us to gain the right perspective. And lead us on the correct path.

We become burned out, exhausted, and bored with our lives, and are tempted to make changes that the Holy Spirit never requested. Our reasoning and justifications too often come from what we see, and worldly information guides us to incorrect decisions.

These steps represent our own desires and assumptions, or good works that we feel will help us get ahead. Even sometimes things we imagine must be done. In our logic, we quickly reason through situations, and reach conclusions that they should take place. Yet things continue to falter and do not seem to work out. Absent of a true relationship with God, we become frustrated attempting to make correct decisions. Then, we realize we are powerless when fighting for control.

True commitment takes surrender and action steps of faith. This promotes trust of God to guide where we should go. Authenticity in this realm is important, as is a steadfast course. The latter is often difficult. We can get distracted for several reasons. God knew we would face temptations and realizes the difficulties. Jesus experienced the same on Earth.

Although we may waiver, the decisions that ultimately reflect our faith in God will increase our commitment and encourage steps in his will. With correct perspective, we realize that temptations are not necessarily negative. They allow opportunities to display our true hearts—and dedication—to God. While this may be difficult, overcoming can bring strength and increased character. "Look to the Lord and his strength; seek his face always" (1 Chr 16:11).

As we unpack the concept of commitment, it should be mentioned that we often have the best intentions. But these may not serve us well. We reflect on situations in which we choose steps that we believe are honoring to God. We base this on what we have been told by others. Or what we have been taught to do. It is important to explore our steps and the true heart behind them. We should spend time listening to the Holy Spirit prior to making any move.

The solution is different for each of us and cannot be collectively declared. A group of people will not walk out God's plan in the exact same manner. Since we each come from a different place, and have varied stories, our individual relationships will not look the same. But God brings people together for a variety of reasons. There should be an authentic commitment from each that promotes personal guidance. Not one to be assumed as the standard or placed on display.

Isaiah 29:13 describes a view of a misguided and artificial relationship. "These people come near to me with their mouth and honor me with their lips, but their hearts are far from me. Their worship of me is based on merely human rules they have been taught." This can happen when we gather in groups and follow the crowd.

We excel, learn, and strengthen when we join in community with like-minded people. However, this should never be misconstrued as having the same plan. Or that guidance from someone other than God should ultimately lead our way.

While it is important to gather with other believers, we should not act only on their requests, or operate under the premise of appeal to their needs. We strive to follow the purpose that God has for us. There should be caution taken and discernment used to maintain this.

It is all too common that we operate on highs when people complement our following of God or feel judgment by those that critique things needing correction. However, our guidance should come only from the Holy Spirit as we build an authentic relationship. This commitment leads our growth with God. And it is the preference over seeking reward for performance or pleasing others for the wrong reasons.

Encouragement

ALTHOUGH WE WILLINGLY ALLOW God into our lives, it is evident that he invited us into his long ago. God still works miracles, mends hearts, encourages minds, and delivers peace. Even if we do not fully understand the possibilities he presents, it only takes hope to believe that these circumstances can happen.

Once our Father has an invitation into our hearts, he begins to display greatness that we could only imagine. God has granted us victory. We only need to believe it, and maintain a stance with him that allows our situations to flourish.

God has amazing blessings in store for us, but the enemy tries to steal our joy and disrupt accomplishments and relationships. God's Word teaches guidelines which combat the lies used by the enemy to render us ineffective.

The devil tells us that we *can't*. Which reflects reminders of the past where we have fallen short. Also, that we *won't*. Which maintains a defeated mindset for the future. In addition, he attempts to convince us that we *aren't* loved. Which breeds lack of hope, ability, and action.

But God provides an alternate view and displays the truths that we believe. We stay encouraged and guard our minds and hearts against the lies of the devil. Where the enemy says we cannot, God tells us we *can* do all things through him because he strengthens us. Instead of saying we will not, God teaches us we *will* because we are prepared overcomers. The father of lies tells us we are not loved. But God says we *are* dearly loved, made in his image, anointed, blessed, and highly favored. We walk in victory with minds of Christ.

We were never expected to make correct choices every time. Instead, to do our best in an authentic relationship with God. We are equipped by him to have every gift and characteristic that we need to accomplish our purpose. But often we have a plethora of reasons why we are unable to take steps.

God equipped us for the call we have in him. We are not expected to be perfect, only willing. We hear from the Spirit of God and believe his truths. This allows open doors for us to walk the intended path. Willingness births opportunities, even if we do not yet know the results or the entire plan.

"Have I not commanded you? Be strong and courageous. Do not be afraid; do not be discouraged, for the Lord your God will be with you wherever you go" (Josh 1:9).

We have learned that an authentic relationship is what God desires. He encourages us to make choices and take steps to continue progression. We have many tools which can be utilized. Even contributions that have not yet been introduced. Only God knows the timeline for each.

Often, we become disengaged because we have strayed from the path that God intended. We might have veered off course. Perhaps we did not clearly hear God's voice. Maybe we were entirely focused on the volume and distractions of the world.

When this happens, we frequently demean ourselves. We tend to forget the enemy continuously attempts to harass us. He strives to lead us to wrong decisions. He promotes missteps from our purposes by lying, cheating, stealing, flaunting, tempting, and ruining our steps as frequently as possible.

We fail often, but God can always redeem. 2 Corinthians chapter 7 in the New Living Translation tells us, "For the kind of sorrow God wants us to experience leads away from sin and results in salvation. There is no regret for that kind of sorrow. But worldly sorrow—which lacks repentance—results in spiritual death" (v. 10). God does not want us to be caught in a whirlwind cycle of shame and disappointment. Or to spend time depleting our worth to him. We often perseverate on deciphering what went wrong or using our own abilities to attempt to remedy issues. Instead, God teaches us to rely on him. We repent to receive forgiveness and guidance.

Through trust that our Father knows all, and his Word is true, we walk joyfully and confidently daily. Even when the world appears to be crumbling around us, his power can accomplish all things. We have faith that God's will is divine. He never promised this journey would be easy. And we maintain that he understands our downfalls and miscues. God is always faithful. We simply turn to him.

Communication

We have discussed gaining power by remaining close to God and relying on his guidance. One of the most essential steps in initiating—and especially in maintaining—a solid relationship is communication. But we often feel unheard or unable to reach God because we cannot see him. Fortunately, this is far from the truth.

Our Father made a way for greater communication when he sacrificed his only son Jesus on the cross. Once Jesus conquered death, it provided the ability to for us to maintain a face-to-face relationship with God.

We speak to him through prayer. We pray directly to God, which is simply talking to him about our lives, and Jesus intercedes. We will be forever grateful for what he has done to allow our freedom. We realize God is not distant. The amazing act permitted a direct line to our Father.

When praying, people often attempt to determine specific formulas or techniques. But God simply wants our hearts. He prefers quality and authenticity over methodology. Our Father desires to be our best friend and confidant. God wants us to be comfortable approaching him quickly and frequently. Even for the smallest situations. Prayer is a conversation by which we invite God into our lives regularly. It is not intended to be escalated into a process that discourages use.

Often, we forfeit talking to our Father because we are convinced it should be time-consuming and specific. Or that perhaps he does not hear us. But we are assured in the Bible that God hears all that we think and speak. He already knows before we say anything. However, he desires that we come to him for development of a close relationship. Therefore, we should never try to hide, but present everything in our hearts. "This is the confidence we have in approaching God: that if we ask anything according to his will, he hears us" (1 John 5:14).

We have more access to God than we realize. We do not have to wait for group gatherings, to be led by others, or to spend time around someone else that prays. He does not judge our communication when we proceed with authentic hearts. God wants us to realize the opportunities he has granted.

Along with a direct line of communication, we see in God's Word that he desires for us to gain wisdom and rely on him, and in turn spread what we learn to others. God is faithful in keeping his Word. He promises that he will reveal the way to life everlasting. But our path should not end with that sentiment. Frankly, it should be the beginning.

Our Father is well-pleased when we draw near. It presents the opportunity for him to teach us amazing concepts which otherwise we would not learn or accomplish. But his true heart is for those who do not yet know him. This is where we discover our initial assignment from God.

Once we have moved into a life of intimacy with him, God asks that we share his goodness with others. Often this creates fear due to mindsets that exist regarding our inabilities. However, there is no expectation for each person to become a profound instructor, preach from the highest pulpit, or even to teach to massive groups. But God has equipped us to spread his promises to those around us.

A sentiment of doubt may enter regarding our abilities to walk this out. However, God grants not only ability, but authority, to share his Word. He instructs that we will have guidance and of course that we are never alone. "For the Holy Spirit will teach you at that time what you should say" (Luke 12:12).

Many see the Great Commission as a call for those in ministry; only for whom they consider the most elite to God. However, his Word teaches that we are all ministers. Once we know our Father, we speak of his amazing ways and what he has to offer. Lives are changed in an instant simply by committing to him.

In the words of Jesus in John chapter 20, "Peace be with you! As the Father has sent me, I am sending you" (v. 21). Imagine how widespread the gospel could become if each of us commits to sharing.

We do not have to be perfect, only willing. When we surrender our shortcomings, communicate with God, and stand open to his call, it propels forth his intention. Which is that we become the body of Christ.

God equips us and uses those things that we consider deficiencies to make us relatable, empathetic, and effective. Our light for God can ignite others when we engage and encourage them. It creates a chain reaction that can deliver the light of Jesus to the world. We need only be willing.

Characteristics

Above all else, guard your heart,
for everything you do flows from it.

PROVERBS 4:23

Pride

PEOPLE OFTEN CONSIDER PRIDE to be an attitude of superiority. A comparison to the knowledge that others lack on subjects, methods, or abilities. It is regarded as an overbearing viewpoint. In this description, pride takes the form of a down-turning opinion of those who are not as elevated or capable.

There are variations of this outlook. But most often pride is considered a version of this sentiment. However, this perspective is only a portion of how pride will be explained. We will view pride as the mindset we exhibit when we attempt our decisions and choices without the guidance of the Holy Spirit. Or input from God.

We have discussed the importance and necessity of remaining surrendered and allowing the Holy Spirit to lead us on a journey with our Father. However, when daily situations arise, we make rapid decisions within the judgment of our desires. But when we take steps without consulting the Spirit of God, we have decided that our abilities prevail above his knowledge and intent.

Even in our daily steps, we may succumb to the demands of the world. We act based on what we assume are best decisions, which often lead to difficult outcomes or misdirection. This goes beyond having confidence in our abilities. Then, we wonder why things seem hard.

This type of thought process can draw us away from God and his benefits. It births "I have it taken care of" mindsets. It can even lead us to believe that certain things do not pertain to us because we are beyond concern of them, or that we are unavailable for interruptions due to our perceived status of self.

A vision of overachievement can bring forth a view of "pedestal versus platform." We undeservingly elevate ourselves. Instead of utilizing our position as a platform to spread light to others. Perhaps we should use our abilities to speak to the greatness of God instead of placing ourselves where he should rightfully be.

On the other hand, a prideful stance is achieved if we untruthfully portray our positions as sufficient when they are not. We may relay that things are fine when we are silently suffering or struggling. This is also a form of pride: still handling circumstances without assistance because we have them covered, but for a different reason. We desire to portray how capable we are within our own abilities, even if we do not believe it.

This type of pride can lead to inability to receive all that God intends. Perhaps we feel he would never choose us, so we are unable to benefit from his goodness. Our sentiments are that we are not good enough, or do not perform well, or that we have not given or done an adequate amount. Even that we do not have sufficient favor.

Both prideful ends of the spectrum lead to attitudes that keep us excluded from relationships with God and others. Excuses and justifications abound in these situations as to why we operate how we do. We have superior or inferior views of self that inhibit growth or our abilities to operate in the likeness of God. We easily create reasons as to how we handle things without assistance. Or why God cannot bless or use us.

Being prideful causes vicious cycles that can be difficult to break. It leads to emotions and characteristics that keep us spinning out of control. Shame is often accompanied with pride in a cyclic manner. This is because shame causes pride, and pride also gives rise to shame. Then we land on a route to isolation. We justify our actions and exclude ourselves from the promises of God. Based on our imaginary standards of measure, we will not receive help because we are undeserving. Or our mindsets are such that we do not need his help anyway.

Some reactions of pride that render us ineffective are as follows: it traps us in our same worn-out methods; we feel as though we must stay in control; it keeps us from recognition of circumstances in true form; and pride can inhibit us from admitting shame to God and others.

These lies of the enemy create steps that keep us imprisoned in a realm where our thoughts become tainted. And it is difficult to stay on track. This encourages constant distraction from where we should be.

But God knows. He designed a way to remedy this. Our Great Counselor—the Holy Spirit—has been positioned to assist us through tumultuous times. Psalm 139 shows us to ask the Spirit to "Search me, God, and know my heart; test me and know my anxious thoughts. See if there is any offensive way in me, and lead me in the way everlasting" (vv. 23–24).

If we humble ourselves and invite him, this will take place. We begin to replay manipulative situations that have formed our mindsets that we realize are not of God. Areas where pride has crept in and overtaken will surface. When we exhibit this posture, God has room to renew our souls.

Losing our prideful stances and gaining faith in God's promises keeps us moving on correct paths and in the right direction. Our surrender promotes full capacity for God to move and for his Spirit to guide us. We realize dependence on God is the only accepted posture.

Humility

Multiple places in Scripture teach that humility invites honor. In James, it is written, "Humble yourselves before the Lord, and he will exalt you" (4:10). Jesus clearly modeled humility in many ways when he was on Earth. None were so evident as when he became our sacrificial lamb on the cross.

What should we recognize about presenting ourselves in a humble manner? Most importantly, that humility is represented when we place the needs of others before our own. Humble people pursue ways to add value to others rather than themselves.

In addition to the actions that represent humility, there are many virtues that accompany it. Patience, joy, kindness, honesty, and consideration, to name a few. On the other hand, lack of humility can bring forth disdain, pride, narcissism, haughtiness, and cruelty.

This characteristic is often difficult to maintain, and we may waiver at times when facing challenges. Or feel as though we are being pulled into temptation. Choosing to be humble takes discipline and will be rewarded by God. Or if overlooked, its absence can usher in struggles.

God never asked us to discern or maneuver this alone. He is near, and we invite his guidance. Humility is a prerequisite for surrender. We resist God when we do not humble ourselves to his role as the Author and the Finisher. Once we commit to stay in a posture of humility, we gain wisdom of the steps that he has prepared.

Our Father will not fight us for control. Staying humble shows God that we value him and will surrender and choose obedience to his conclusion. In essence, that we trust what he offers is more pertinent than our own agendas.

Humility brings forth the realization that we do not possess the answers, but that God is truly our Source. When we falter and move from a place of surrender, there is often an assumption that we hold more knowledge, or that we have everything under control. This perception leads to pride.

God gave us free will to allow opportunities for decisions and to follow him. We more easily hear his voice if we approach with a posture of humility. As James said, "He will exalt you" (4:10).

This means that God views us as trustworthy to walk out the intentions he has ordained. We grant him access and agree to follow his lead. Only then is he able to guide and utilize us to the fullest capacity.

So why do we find it difficult to remain humble? Often, we are tempted to believe there is weakness in conceding to others. Or that we are deserving of objects or ideas which gives us a false sense of ownership. We should remember that the world does not fulfill our needs.

When we yield to this realm of deceit, the basis of our success is skewed by incorrect views. It may take the form of material items, misplaced leadership, or even the desire to have control of situations and relationships. Humility cannot exist in these impulsive steps which only deliver arrogance. "Do nothing from rivalry or conceit, but in humility count others more significant than yourselves" (Phil 2:3).

All too often we justify decisions. We assume that we will be better off utilizing our own powers or feel the need to gain what we desire. These urges will be stifled as we alter our path with more reliance on God. As we submit, and allow him to move in our situations, he will teach us correct steps. Humble hearts will bring forth wisdom from our Father.

When we maintain that our kinship is with God—and that he has adopted us as his children—we desire a close and humble relationship with him. We honor what the Bible shows us and view it as our sole truth. We worship God humbly with whole hearts, so that we grow in his likeness. And we stay encouraged realizing he has granted us the victory of eternity.

Love

One of the most identified fruits of the Holy Spirit is love. Our perspective is that it can deliver joy or sorrow, depending on circumstances. Love can birth a feeling of elation or may readily lead to depths of pain. Especially if we experience disappointments from those we greatly care about.

This description of love is based on what society associates with reality. But here we will focus on true love. The love of our Savior. Our one true God. He showed unsurpassed intimacy when he ordained Jesus to die on the cross for our sins. An unselfish act of love which we will not discover in the ups and downs of this world. And that certainly cannot be established by other people.

Our level of love is often measured by reflections of the way we are treated or according to circumstances between us. In essence how we *feel*. But instead of an emotion, we will consider love a virtue that we choose. For example, by nature we are more tolerant of downfalls with family members. We experience a deeper love for them versus those that are infrequent guests. However, we can choose authentic love rather than wait to feel loving.

Unfortunately, because we experience emotional love more regularly, we frequently love God in the same manner as we love people: based on their treatment of us, or reactions that we have encountered with them. If we reach out to God and feel he does not respond, we may retreat as a method of protection or even out of frustration. But God never falls away. His "love never fails," as his Word states (1 Cor 13:8).

Verses 4–7 show the ideal that is God's love. We often assume that we have the capacity to maintain the same—or that others should—but it is a model as to how we strive to love one another. However, only God accomplishes this perfectly every time. He teaches that love is tolerant and kind. It is not jealous, boastful, or proud. Also, that love does not dishonor, encourage anger, remember offenses, and is not selfish. Love discourages evil and desires to always deliver truth, protection, trust, hope and perseverance.

Perhaps there is an assumption that we possess many qualities of love when we genuinely care for someone. But God requests that we love *all* people in this manner regardless of circumstance. While God challenges us to love our neighbor, he does not express that we must like or accept everything that they represent.

Logically, we would presume that God was displeased with the acts of his people when they mistrusted, fought, and dishonored him and each other. Or when they betrayed and crucified him. But thankfully, Jesus displayed that his love for us is unconditional. He conquered death when we were still sinners to grant a way to everlasting life. An act of true love; one we are extremely grateful that he did not wait on us to deserve.

Jesus' model of love teaches us how we are called to extend this gesture. Just as he chose to fulfill destiny on the cross because of his devotion to us, we choose to spread love to others. We do not wait until we feel they are justified in receipt of our endearment, or feel that they have earned our adoration. This especially pertains to those that have wronged or harmed us. Although seemingly impossible at times, this is God's desire.

When we surrender to his will, and realize he is the Messiah, we begin to view others with the light and affection which God does. This is a certain and true way to extend love to all people. Even if we have not yet achieved this due to the actions or mindsets of individuals, we turn to God and draw even closer. He has taught us nothing is impossible through him.

When referring to our walk, 1 Corinthians 13 describes partial knowledge; thinking like a child; and only seeing a reflection in a mirror. But then it speaks of a "completeness" that comes. This allows the partial knowledge to disappear. The children to become men. And for the reflection to fall away and deliver a face-to-face encounter. This is the dynamic that Jesus delivered through the cross. An expression of true love so our relationship with God could grow in depth, maturity, and closeness. And we would revel in the love that Jesus taught us to express.

One important aspect that must be mentioned is our love for self. Not love *of* self in a righteous or boastful manner. But rather a love *for* self because we belong to our Father. We are his beloved and he adores us. However, too often we have disdainful views of ourselves. Maybe these are based on incorrect decisions, past or present actions, or appearances. God's desire is for us to capture the realization of the way he sees us and that we maintain the same perspective.

Our Father loves us dearly. He made us in his image. It grieves God when we possess a lowly view of self. Or when we feel incapable, unlovable, or unable to stay in relationship with him. These misconceptions are the most conniving lies of the enemy. They are used to keep us far from God. And to launch a posture of isolation.

Jesus sacrificed so that we may live. This includes the foundational truth that "We love because He first loved us" (1 John 4:19). The love God wants us to experience includes love for self. No matter what has happened in previous encounters. In addition, God desires we walk out a Christ-like relationship with others. Filled with the same authentic love he first showed us.

Peace

In a world where many distractions and disruptions take place—with less than satisfactory outcomes—a peaceful mind and spirit can be difficult to maintain. Spiritual peace takes daily observance and continued surrender. We request God's assistance to locate and experience a correct state.

We begin by identifying true peace. This view does not represent quiet, tranquility, stillness, rest, or calm. But instead, an overall wholeness and state of oneness with God. His Word tells us that he is the Author of Peace. Also, that he can bring forth a peace that exceeds all comprehension. But worldly peace is described much differently. Society considers peace the absence of turmoil.

While peace is often accompanied by specific terms, none individually represent the peace of God. Instead, it is an encompassing fruit brought only by his Spirit. We cannot accomplish this type of peace on our own. And we certainly cannot locate it in the world.

God intends for us to walk in peace during both our complicated and celebrated times. We succeed by trusting him and believing that only he can grant us solace. The Holy Spirit escorts us to a place of peace when we are surrendered to him. We cannot achieve this through our own strengths or abilities. It is a part of God.

Perhaps we have experienced difficulties that include traumatic life events. A relationship breach, sadness from circumstances, a physical ailment, financial woes, and even loss from death. Only God can bring us to a peaceful state of fulfillment by his power.

And included is the security that only he can provide. God grants increased peace when we relinquish our own expectations.

This is regularly a challenge because the enemy generates a view of incapability. He wants us to maintain the assumption that we are unable to achieve satisfaction. We often take a personal stance, and our outlooks become filled with failure. The world provides techniques and methods that assure we will arrive at a place of serenity. However, this disappoints time and again.

Then, we assume there is no blame to place other than on self. What we often overlook is that God never intended us to accomplish true peace within our own abilities or by operating against futile attempts. There is another way entirely.

We are eager to receive this benefit, and readily can because we believe God's promises are true. But we must arrive at the understanding that we do not have the mental, emotional, or physical capacities to single-handedly maintain this state. "You will keep in perfect peace those whose minds are steadfast, because they trust" (Isa 26:3).

Once we turn to the Holy Spirit to seek authentic peace, we invite his potency into our circumstances. This strength continues as we remain surrendered and sustain from an accurate source. When we rely on him, God will never let us down. When we walk in this faith, it will alter our outlooks. It even ushers in identification of realms. We have the capacity to distinguish Earthly versus heavenly. And we achieve true joy.

We arrive at the comprehension that a closeness with God increases our trust in him. This ultimately translates to a rise in faith. It allows assistance while coming to terms regarding inner struggles, which are often the culprit of difficult, daily life situations. Past and present. We adopt alternate views of our shortcomings and become more tolerant due to peace from God's Spirit.

By remaining joined with him, we also gain a relationship that promotes less distractions and greater desire to adhere to the intended course. Our gratitude will grow. Not only for God, but for those around us. We will realize the importance of dependence on our Father, which promotes humility toward him. Peace is discovered in faith-filled steps.

After reviewing the stages and guidelines, it is important to remember that peace is a choice. Most often, we find downfall in this view. We try to command ourselves to feel peaceful. However, understanding that it is only initiated through God magnifies the realization that we choose peace when we choose God. We cannot reach an authentic peace alone.

In John, the Word tells us that we can believe we will have peace even with tribulations because Jesus has overcome the world. The fact that the most tragic event in history is the very same that delivers us—and brings ultimate peace—can only be ordained by God. By Jesus dying on the cross, he developed a direct connection to our Father. This promotes discovery of the wholeness and completeness of his peace. We experience his serenity and righteousness. True peace only in the presence of God.

He desires to grant this peace and invites us into a place of unity. "Now may the Lord of peace himself give you peace at all times in every way. The Lord be with you all" (2 Thess 3:16).

Patience

When contemplating the word patience, it brings forth the image of waiting or withstanding a situation. We often declare the need for increased patience when dealing with difficulties, people, or when facing certain conditions.

When envisioning patience in a worldly realm, it entails the act of monitoring time. And our tolerance. However, a heavenly version does not encompass simply enduring, but operating well. It includes encountering and experiencing many aspects during the journey.

Daily, we focus on the tasks at hand and perceive how to maneuver through. We might even attempt to determine an amount of time each will require and are hopeful for a shorter duration. This mindset pertains to a variety of circumstances we address in life. We easily fall into habitual ruts hoping for just enough tolerance to make it through. Then we look up only to realize that the substance of life is passing us by.

Depending on the length of time involved, some situations generate more challenges. Even a short period can be taxing. How we handle these steps determines our true measure of patience. Are our actions graceful and kind? Or perhaps they are they filled with frustration and intolerance. How can we display true ability to handle things smoothly?

One solution is to focus less on ourselves and more on others. When we exhibit humility and desire to put the needs of others before ours, they become the center of attention. As we follow through with this viewpoint, we are much less likely to perseverate on what may be causing difficulties in our own lives.

Once we begin to change our motivation, there are aspects that lead to heightened value. It allows a lesser magnification of our own issues and a greater focus on occurrences that bring joy. This is one virtue that leads to a more patient character. Once we adjust our central focus, we can walk in a place of peaceful satisfaction and often a more restful state of mind.

Our joy is not due to feelings of happiness. True joy is from within our spirits. We choose joy because of what Jesus accomplished on the cross. It is a reminder that we are walking in victory because he conquered the world. When authentic, it can be experienced even when we are dealing with difficult situations. Instead of being tossed around by the storms of life, we stand patiently in the face of adversities.

Those that are deeply rooted in our Father maintain true joy. He is our Source. Once we trust him to assist, lead, and protect in all times of need, we relinquish the control of steering and instead desire to be guided by correct steps.

As with many aspects, if we arrive at the dedication to lead—instead of choosing faith in God—we reach endings in which we were never intended to exist. Not only does patience become more challenging, but we are more heavily weighted. When we allow the burden of expectation to be lifted, only then can we experience a realm in which we have true reliance on God. And in his ability to always know what is right.

In Exodus 14, God teaches that he will go to battle for us when we are still. (v. 14). This means that when we surrender, and relinquish the reins, he will guide. Staying in his will brings peace and joy. This promotes patience because we surrender the requirement to control our waiting and situations in general. This holds true, no matter the amount of time involved. But it requires a close relationship and reliance on God.

In addition to our patience for the things of this world, we will address our patience for God. As Christians, we desire to spend our days pleasing the Lord and waiting well for his return to Earth. This not only pertains to occasional circumstances but is the overview until we see Jesus again.

We normally judge patience on the way we handle instances and people. But how do we fare when it comes to God? When we have been believing and praying and have not yet received? Are we able to wait patiently while walking joyfully? Or are we overcome with emotions of confusion—or even frustration—when we assume God does not hear us?

Our Father's Word teaches that he never abandons us and that just as he began a good work in us, he will see it to completion. Also, that God's timing is always perfect. So, we should not mistake God's occasional silence for his absence. He is always nearby.

Romans 8 clearly states, "But if we hope for what we do not see, through perseverance we wait eagerly for it" (v. 25). This tells us to remain hopeful and enthusiastic for the Lord and to stay vigilant to his answers and lessons.

We should never hesitate to call out to God or draw near to him. Instead, we believe that he has the capacity to lead us to a more patient character. As we have learned, God is a faithful Father and loves us dearly. He wants only the best for us and does not provide in halfway measures.

We hold the knowledge that we were made in his image. And when we remain in his likeness, we maneuver through our waiting periods and circumstances well. With grace and a joyful outlook.

Kindness

ALONG WITH LOVE, JOY, peace, and patience, kindness is a fruit of the Holy Spirit. It leads to compassion and consideration for others. It brings forth assistance and generosity; perhaps of time or ability. Kindness is a choice. And it begins with humility.

This virtue has sometimes been mistaken for meekness or weakness. There is a sentiment that extended kindness equals being taken advantage of. Or that perhaps it involves a mindset of inferiority versus those who stand their ground and demand what they want.

In truth, kindness is an action chosen when convicted to share our light and love. Displaying acts of kindness requires more strength and self-control than reactions of satisfaction or self-promotion.

In addition, gentleness exists when we show kindness to others. There is power in thoughtful steps and in choosing the correct path. And discipline is displayed when we take this initiative with others.

Jesus showed much kindness in his time on Earth and was rich in compassion to those around him. This was clearly displayed when he cried out to God from his position on the cross, "Father, forgive them, for they do not know what they are doing" (Luke 23:34). Even in his angst, Jesus was petitioning for us. The very ones who created his dismal situation.

As with love, we often judge if people are worthy of our kindness. We may choose compassion when we have been treated well, or in return for other acts that have been expressed. But not necessarily in an unconditional manner as Jesus modeled.

God uses the Holy Spirit to convict our hearts to desire the spread of compassion, even when we may not feel like following through. As a true spiritual advocate, he promotes choosing kindness especially when someone is undeserving, not only when we deem it appropriate by our own authority.

In fact, kindness should not be underestimated. A gesture driven by our light—and ordained by God—can turn even the iciest heart to flesh. Who will bring change to the world if not us?

We may never know the circumstances that someone is facing. However, if we extend our reach to touch them with compassion and kindness—and in a considerate manner—it creates a lasting effect. We might not even realize the full extent. Often, we are the only touch from Jesus that people may experience. If we commit to kindness, imagine the impact it could have in our vicinity. And to the world.

A gentle nature toward others can spring forth an effect of how those they next encounter are treated. Having generosity with our time and treasures has lasting results on others, even when we may not witness the outcome. The choice to spend a few extra moments could change someone's day and maybe even their life.

In addition, goodness is another fruit of the Spirit. These two virtues are often incorrectly interchanged. Just as the act of being nice does not correlate with virtue-driven kindness, goodness has its own guidelines.

Goodness is considered to be taking action to do the moral and correct thing as designed by God's righteousness. We are not capable of holding this position alone. By the sacrifice of Jesus, we walk in righteousness. But only through him. Goodness comes forth when we stay surrendered to the will of God and allow him to teach us the way of spreading light in an ideal manner.

Both kindness and goodness are fruits of the Spirit. We should pray for guidance of them during our daily walk. Showing generosity and spreading compassion—while treating others with gentleness and consideration—is the virtue of kindness. When we invite Jesus into our lives, he will lead us into righteous actions and choices. This is goodness.

We choose kindness because we love Jesus and want to stay in his likeness. When he lives in us, the desire grows. If we remain close to God, it promotes the kingdom of heaven to come near. And allows more ease in walking this into completion.

Because we love him, we attempt to stay pleasing to God. And we desire to spread his love to others. This is shown in Colossians 3:12 which states, "So, as those who have been chosen of God, holy and beloved, put on a heart of compassion, kindness, humility, gentleness and patience."

We operate by the model that Jesus displayed on Earth. And we rely on the guidance of the Holy Spirit for conviction of steps. Recalling that it is a choice to share these fruits allows a confident path for virtuous encounters.

Wisdom

As with many topics we have discussed, wisdom is gained when we grow closer to God. To experience authentic and Godly wisdom, we pray to hear him and desire to listen to what he is teaching. It is experienced through a true relationship, not because we feel smarter by simply gaining information. Wisdom is a gift of the Holy Spirit.

There are ideas and solutions we learn from those around us and from what we see. This is worldly knowledge. It should not be mistaken for the wisdom that comes from the heavenly realm. The Holy Spirit teaches us all we need to know from God.

True Godly wisdom will not only lift us up, but it also sustains us. As we remain open to continuous communication with God, he imparts wisdom. He relies on us to utilize this information in the correct manner.

When we are in a relationship with our Father, he graciously shares wisdom. We need only ask, as it tells us in James 1:5: "If any of you lacks wisdom, you should ask God, who gives generously to all without finding fault, and it will be given to you."

This clearly portrays that wisdom is available to everyone. When we reach out to God, he gifts us with those things we require to live for him. If we are willing, and believe that he will move in this, his Word shows us that he is faithful. His desire is for us to gain greater understanding of who he is and likewise share this with others.

God does not randomly grant pieces of nonsensical information. Instead, he brings forth wisdom that we need for success. And at the perfect time. Like a savory recipe, the ingredients come together to create an amazing masterpiece. And each portion provides its own contribution. God delivers on his promises.

In addition comes revelation. This is the method by which God imparts his wisdom and shares his desires. When we receive revelation, it grants deeper comprehension of God's heart and his intentions. Wisdom and revelation move in conjunction, which can be seen in Ephesians chapter 1. "I keep asking that the God of our Lord Jesus Christ, the glorious Father, may give you the Spirit of wisdom and revelation, so that you may know him better" (v. 17). Paul continues in verse 18 speaking about the enlightenment of our hearts which can bring hope and "the riches of his glorious inheritance."

Just as there is a difference in worldly wisdom and that from our Savior, so is the idea behind revelation. The world may reveal information and display cultural ideas that were previously unknown. We learn these as we journey through life. This is often a mechanism for survival. But authentic enlightenment allows us to thrive.

Revelation from the Spirit unlocks details and content that are already present. We have simply been blind to them previously as the timing was not right. Ideas and information are revealed to our conscious minds that were already familiar within our spirits. The true concept of emergence. We will review what God's Word teaches so that we can gain further understanding of this view.

Full disclosure is written in Ephesians 1:3–14. It explains that God chose us at the beginning of time. God knew he would send his son Jesus to be our hope and our Savior. And only through this blameless sacrifice would we be brought into kinship and adoption with God. He redeemed us by Jesus' blood. He lavished us with riches and promised wisdom that could only be understood once Jesus fulfilled his destiny. Through Jesus, God reveals his will.

It is a simple yet powerful truth. We were already equipped with all that we need to survive and thrive. God knew us before we were ever formed. We were born with giftings and abilities, but

God allows them to flourish as we mature in our relationship. And when the time is right—per his infinite wisdom—we grow more reliable to God. This unity happens when we stay aligned and believe. We gain wisdom through revelation and can utilize the gifts that God has placed within us.

Once we have received God's wisdom, we are called to nurture our spirits. Much like we would care for a garden. There is a necessity for prepared soil—followed by sufficient nutrition—to encourage seedlings to sprout. Then light, and continued nourishment, are needed to increase growth. The elimination of weeds and other corruption of the foundation is necessary.

Just as we can be filled, our spirits may also move to a state of depletion. Most often this happens through worldly distractions, circumstances that lead us away from where we were originally intended to be, like an empty gas tank that causes a car to stall and not proceed. But we can be replenished by recognizing God as our Source of all things. Our foundation with him is vital and must remain solid. Because although we can pour into an empty gas tank, it will never remain filled if there is a leak.

We have more impact with Godly wisdom when we are proactive. We have been taught by the Word of God to ask the Holy Spirit to identify any deficits so that we may remedy these to gain wisdom and revelation. As we walk in humility, and take time to grow closer to our Father, he is faithful to show us the way.

There are three easy steps for this development. We grow closer to God by spending time in worship and allowing him to encompass our praise. With worship we grow in reverence and honor of God as our King. We pray, which is simply having conversation with God about any and everything. With prayer we grow in strength and trust of God. We also study his Word to grow closer. The Word brings forth power and understanding. "So then faith comes by hearing, and hearing by the word of God" (Rom 10:17).

Reading the Bible may seem difficult. And it can be challenging to study God's Word. This is the mindset the enemy wants us to maintain. He strives to keep us from realizing our power and authority. The devil is fearful of increased knowledge and understanding. And even more so when we gain wisdom and revelation. Even still, we hesitate at times regarding our next steps. God holds promises for this. "Your words have supported those who stumbled; you have strengthened faltering knees" (Job 4:4).

We will focus on the best methods for studying the Word. It must be mentioned that each person will hear differently and can discern through the Holy Spirit what is being spoken to them. But instead of viewing the Bible as a book—simply picking it up to read—begin to perceive the Word as a living entity with interactive messages directly from God that pertain to our lives.

Spend a few moments in prayer asking God for hunger of his Word and motivation prior to reading. God loves our willing hearts and will honor this if we ask. An additional step, as we lean into Scripture, is to petition God for magnification of his desires and all that he wants us to comprehend. We can also request clarity as we study the Bible to discern God's intentions and promises.

Finally, we should trust God for wisdom of action steps. "I will instruct you and teach you in the way you should go; I will counsel you with my loving eye on you" (Ps 32:8). God is faithful in maturing our walk. And his Word is how he accomplishes this. It covers all that God wants to teach us. We only need to stay willing and committed. We ask him to prepare and guide us during the journey.

Emotions

Take my yoke upon you and learn from me,
for I am gentle and humble in heart,
and you will find rest for your souls.

MATTHEW 11:29

Hurt

Emotions are often identified simply as feelings. But emotions stem from thoughts, memories, circumstances, experiences, and sensations. They drive us to ups and downs. Sometimes into difficulties. Emotions can cause much unsteadiness.

When they surface, emotions are accompanied by actions. And in turn, those actions create reactions. Once we operate in this realm, habitual actions become a part of us. They even alter our character and cause transformation of our views.

Hurt is an emotion with numerous sources. It encompasses broad categories and can surface in a variety of areas. Possibly from broken promises, mistrust caused by untruths, or unmet physical needs. And these are only a few examples. Our history might be riddled with instances that have caused emotional pain and scars.

When we experience hurt, it can lead to distraught feelings and loneliness. Next comes the position of isolation rather than facing more hurt. Although the circumstances are different, the emotion that accompanies them is familiar.

Perhaps we have experienced hurt more than once, or more frequently than we prefer to admit. This ushers in the idea of seclusion. Excess time is spent replaying the situation and reliving the hurt multiple times over. We end up on a merry-go-round of emotions with an even more negative impact. Hurt is a powerful entity.

How do we overcome hurt that people cause? Or stop the feeling of isolation when we have experienced this cycle? At our core, we were made with a desire for relationship. However, the very structure that feeds us can also generate starvation.

Our emotional state is often directly correlated with how people treat us. It is tied to actions and reactions in those moments. When reflecting on disagreement, it is sometimes evident that this does not begin as a direct challenge or a sense of frustration. But it can frequently end in this manner. Why do our steps lead to such difficult outcomes?

Often, hurt is initiated from unmet expectations. Our expectations are a driving force for what we think and how we react. But our expectations are sometimes not attainable. In essence, they are the difference in how we perceive things *should* be and how things actually *are*. Maybe even falling into the scope of how we wish things could be.

This is true in multiple situations: with a spouse, at work, school, and with children. And it can take place in most any realm. We desire our thoughts to play out in reality. Unfortunately, this involves not only us, but other people. And it is impossible to control.

A method of surpassing this mindset is to approach each situation with the outlook that people have a variety of views. And we cannot be responsible for their decisions or actions. We can only explain our preferences by communicating our thoughts. But this too can become a point of breakdown. High expectations—with little communication—equal misunderstood consequences.

Only God knows our innermost thoughts, unless we share them honestly and fully with others. Even then, people often misread and incorrectly comprehend. We are unforgiving when this happens. And hurt or even anger forms. But we should attempt to understand that people base views on their mindset and individual experiences. These details are not exactly alike for any two people. Which also promotes confusion and even less empathy.

Recall the explanation of emergence. Specifically, the example of the seed. When an object is nurtured, it grows from darkness to light. This also pertains when addressing those that misunderstand us, or even unlovely people. We do not over-water—dictate only our desires. Or shine too much harsh light—delivery of words and actions matter. But in moderation, the seed remains in the ideal condition to flourish.

God does not operate in extremes, nor does he want us to exist in them. This is where our reliance on him—and his wisdom—is vital. "Wisdom makes one wise person more powerful than ten rulers in a city" (Eccl 7:19).

We allow God to teach what will bring wholeness in situations where we have experienced hurt. He will magnify circumstances as we gain revelation. An increase in gentleness can lead to pardon and grace for others. And for ourselves.

But the enemy prefers we stay hurt, lonely, defeated, and weak. Isolation is one of his most conniving tactics. Because when alone, we cannot hear from others how incredibly equipped we are.

The devil intends for us to continue with feelings of unworthiness. He strives to portray that we cannot gain joy, love, or receive the promises of God. And he will do anything to keep us detached from a relationship that proves otherwise.

Emotions are powerful. If we try to clear our minds, it is possible to perceive we are getting ahead. But there are usually alternate agendas driving our emotions. Memories, situations, and experiences. We find ourselves on an out-of-control roller coaster. But this cycle can be broken. We count on God's accuracy and clarity. His Word will never lead us astray.

His truths become our truths. They are not only authentic occasionally—depending on how we feel—they never change. We can maintain this grasp with assurance. If we stay surrendered to the Almighty, he will encompass our lives and can renew our souls. He will restore us.

Fear

It has been said that Scriptures regarding fear are the most numerous in the Bible. Perhaps because fear is one of the most powerful emotions. It stems from our concerns. The thought that something might happen; that we may be threatened; or that we will possibly experience pain. It encompasses more than one realm. Fear can lead to numerous emotions and actions. Some examples are worry, anxiety, depression, and nervousness. Fear can even cause panic. In addition, there is increased complication because it exhibits differently in each of us.

When we are fearful, we have difficulty seeing clearly. We may perseverate on problems or situations which cause distraction from others, truths, and even from God.

The devil wants us to stay focused on our fear so that it drives our steps into hopelessness and lack of faith. Once this becomes the magnified image, we may question ourselves, our lives, and even God. However, identifying our fear—and perceived inequities—can help lay groundwork for an increased hope and faith.

One common emotion that channels the cycle of fear is worry. But worry is wasted time. We may spend hours, days or even longer contemplating things that *might* happen. We play out the "what ifs" that we envision and never reach an actual conclusion because the thoughts are imagined. Mark Twain said, "I've had a lot of worries in my life, most of which never happened." This is an indication of time spent, in distress, regarding things that never take place.

The Bible tells us not to worry about what is to come, our basic provisions, or how to handle what we say and do. There is no need for concern because God will lead us if we trust him and allow him room for movement. God's Word asks if "any one of you by worrying add a single hour to your life?" (Matt 6:27).

Worry becomes a garment that we wear. Sometimes without even realizing it. And worry can suppress our abilities. Our minds may slip into a spiral of concern. Worry removes our attention from those things that should capture the greatest importance. Over time, focusing on fear can become a habitual distraction. It alters our actions and reactions, and ultimately our character. But we have choices.

If we allow the focus on fear to become larger than our Father, we are unable to stay surrendered to his will. We create gaps in our faith and in our lives. Our hope diminishes. We move into a place of doubt due to the weight of our fear. Over time, an enlarged space emerges between fear and hope. Until it creates an even wider breach in our faith. We remedy this by choosing God and trusting the Holy Spirit to lead us to his fruits.

Instead of believing the enemy's lie that we should be fearful—and that dreadful things will happen—we choose to believe the Word of God. As we draw near to him—and trust that he will keep us from harm—we gain the realization that we possess a major role in our faith. It is our responsibility to step when our Father leads. But through fear, we often become paralyzed when he summons.

Isaiah chapter 43 tells us, "Forget the former things; do not dwell on the past. See, I am doing a new thing! Now it springs up; do you not perceive it? I am making a way in the wilderness and streams in the wasteland" (vv. 18–19). His inquiry about perception beckons the question if perhaps we miss what God is doing. This Scripture challenges us to increase awareness and keep our attention on him, so that our Father can lead.

In further combatting this emotion, we should consider curiosity as the opposite of fear. The notion that faith opposes fear is often expressed. But if we are in a state of hopelessness—and cannot muster even one small step—that concept may pose a distressing challenge. God places curiosity in our hearts, and it draws us away from fear.

Curiosity represents new beginnings and can spring forth action steps, if we choose to take them. When God displays an interest, he is birthing a new idea in us. It can represent a step in overcoming fear. It can begin to heal our situations, relationships, and create a plethora of fresh opportunities. Discernment of this newfound curiosity encourages trustworthiness in God. Ask the Holy Spirit to counsel. And strive to remain close to the Source.

Too often, we do not perceive the curiosity, and do not press in. It remains a fleeting notion and stays buried, instead of the seed of its intention. We spend time discounting the concept and analyzing the reasons we are too afraid to try. We assume that opportunities will not work. And we do not consult God.

However, we can condition ourselves to listen and embrace curiosity. We test our thoughts against God's Word, pray about our steps, and ask the Holy Spirit to lead the way. Leaning into these possibilities shows our obedience.

When we hear from God to move, it is not uncommon to initiate steps with some amount of fear. But our Father helps us overcome. In fact, we usually do not propel forward with progressive steps without some nervous anticipation. However, staying in our comfort zone does not allow growth. Counting on God during this movement brings forth needed assurance.

God desires our trust and our whole hearts. "For the eyes of the Lord range throughout the earth to strengthen those whose hearts are fully committed to him" (2 Chr 16:9).

God is faithful and loves us unconditionally. He designed a way out of the fearful, emotional state that keeps us ineffective. His protection and guidance are available. We only need to choose him. Once we understand our position with God, we realize there is no need to be fearful.

Anxiety

ANXIETY IS A REACTION that results from the emotion of worry. Worry is categorized within the realm of fear. These emotions and reactions are closely related.

When we allow our minds to escalate to a position of worry, we exacerbate the thoughts of what *might* go wrong. When we continue to examine potential outcomes, it plunges us into a place of apprehension. Then, we imagine a variety of conflicts, with additional worry, which invites increased anxiety.

Through these emotions, we remain in a self-centered state. We are solely focused on the possibilities that could be encountered. With increased time in consideration of endings—and contemplations of what may happen—anxiety encompasses multiple areas of our lives. Such as our relationships, responsibilities, and even our excess time.

Once we enter an arena of preoccupations and anxious thoughts, it initiates further distraction. This reaction takes on the form of lingering ideas and devastating assumptions, which inhibits a clear view of the path God intended.

The world quickly leads us astray and into the basis of deceit. As we take each turn, we become more intertwined—and maneuver slowly—in an unsure and tedious manner. We expend much energy worrying and feeling anxious, and basing our actual steps on imagined encounters.

We struggle and experience turmoil because we were never intended to walk in an insecure space. God designed us to operate in his likeness and has granted means to ensure that we do so. Our security is anchored in him. He allows a descent from the escalation of anxious thoughts and overwhelming schemes of the enemy.

One of the primary—yet most powerful—methods that God invites us into is worship. How does this correlate with fear, worry, or even anxiety? God teaches us that there is a glorious exchange that takes place when we approach him with an authentic heart and pure intentions. We experience more of God and less of us. Our mind becomes settled and pure within his covering. Until this occurs, we are hard-pressed to detach or locate an exit from the entrapment of anxious thoughts, or to escape from the cycle of worry once and for all. This was exemplified when Bishop George D. Crenshaw stated, "You can't worry and worship at the same time."

We are called to action to inhibit this emotional state. However, we are often too overburdened by what *might be* to focus on what *actually is*. A small stride in the right direction can deliver freedom and launch the potential to alter our focus on God. As we worship—even if we take one tiny step—God honors our attempt. He moves in our praise, and we experience peace in him.

Although it is comforting to learn that we are not required to make grand gestures, we may still be discouraged due to feeling overburdened. However, God does not leave us in an area of insecurity. He continues the pursuit to rescue us. If we surrender to God's will—and allow movement—he will remove the heavy weights that suppress us.

We also discover rest in realizing that God already knows what we are facing. While he did not ordain steps in anxiety, he understands every thought that occurs in our minds. And each situation that burdens us with stress.

This was modeled in the Bible when David was in anguish and trembling in fear. He was up against destructive forces—and enemies—and was in distress. We see in Psalm 55: 22 that he says, "Cast your cares on the Lord and he will sustain you; he will never let the righteous be shaken."

This verse clearly shows that we can rely on God to overcome our troubles. And that he cares for us. But we often veer from this mindset and envision ourselves as undeserving. Take note of where Psalm 55 shows the Lord protecting the righteous. That refers to us. Although we are unworthy, God created a way by the sacrificial blood of Jesus. We become righteous only through him. Not by our power or of our own accord.

Because God dearly loves us, he planned for our encouragement and assurance. He understands that we require rescue, even from our own perceptions. When we are caught in the snare of deceit—which presses us to remain anxious and afraid—we rely on God for freedom. We draw near to him, surrender, and believe in his abilities. Our Father ushers change into our minds and spirits. We become strong, confident, and composed in his power.

Jealousy

We live in a world where it is easy to witness much of what people do and to envy their possessions. We are obsessed with comparing our abilities, belongings, and situations to that of others. We quickly identify areas in which we feel lack and have difficulty accepting our perceived shortcomings. Urges develop to gain more, and to experience what we assume is missing. Or that which we feel entitled to control.

Perhaps there is insecurity in more than one category. Struggles ensue in many realms when we focus on how people view us. We might have concerns that we are deemed subpar. Or we consider too often how we are treated by others. These impressions are harmful. If they continue over time, they lead to a skewed reality based on untruths. These examples set the stage for jealousy.

It is exhausting to operate from a place of constant inferiority. We develop a lowly view of self which leads to negative emotions and actions. We move in a destructive manner when nudged to perform by what we gather from others.

In addition, we become trapped and allow intentions to lead us astray. We can be propelled down a wrong path solely based on our desperate desire to prove worth. And we feel harassed by situations that pressure and mislead us to a place of deceit.

These methods are distractions from our intended course. They cause confusion and unfulfillment. And can lure us to unrecognizable outcomes, into realms we were never meant to encounter, and a life that feels tedious and burdened. All because we feel the necessity to prove ourselves to those who likely do not notice anyway.

But God—in his infinite wisdom—has the answers and the escape. As we have learned, his intent is to remain in relationship. He discourages our focused concern regarding others' thoughts or judgments. By asking God to examine our hearts, he grants clarity as to our true worth. And our significance. We realize that our desires to covet other things are unnecessary. Instead of continued insecurity, God leads us to a settled and peaceful mindset.

When we step based on proving our abilities and substance, we overlook the objectives God ordained. Jealousy encourages abrupt actions. And incorrect motives often birth false outcomes. When we fail to take the time to consult with God prior to stepping, mistakes are easily made. And we become ensnared by temptation.

"These are the people who divide you, who follow mere natural instincts and do not have the Spirit" (Jude 1:19). The phrase "natural instincts" represents our desires to make decisions and prove ourselves. Instead, we are called to operate from a place of surrender, while relying on the Holy Spirit to guide us. Rather than depend on our personal knowledge, we should trust God's wisdom.

When considering a materialistic view, we often attempt to justify. The possessions we try to acquire may not be in the will of God nor are our intended accomplishments. Instead, we are encouraged to display a posture of humility, and even one of patience. But these expectations are opposite what the world teaches. One of the greatest challenges is to remain surrendered. And to maintain certainty in God's desire and ability to guide our walk.

A display of humility—and one way to await God's counsel—is to grow where we are planted. Reaching a secure stance exactly as we are is difficult, yet powerful. It encourages magnification of gratitude, while escorting in greater acceptance. We enhance this experience by spending time with the Lord and asking him to enlarge our territory. He prepares us for ordained promotion and gain. All in his timing. The key is to step when and where God leads, not as we determine.

Imagine the concept of re-planting a flower. There is a reliance on sturdy roots that have been primed for growth. When transplantation occurs, the movement is not to a pot with smaller area. The root has grown larger and stronger. Therefore, the new location has potential to promote more fruitful development.

In addition, the flower should not surpass the next step and propel forward to the largest container. This would allow increased room for weeds—and overgrowth—and promotes more upkeep. In essence, unneeded responsibilities. Also, more time would be required for the roots to become saturated for optimal growth. If the container is not an accurate fit—too small or too large—it promotes stressors for the plant.

Similarly, we can find ourselves in locations that create pressure. There may be distractions from expectations, and we insist on moving. Or missed opportunities when we remain still. If we intentionally await our Father's guidance—which is anointed and timed impeccably—we are prepared and remain viable. We will not wilt or perish. We can be transplanted, and our foundation will remain intact. Our journey will exhibit more fruitfulness.

In God's eyes, we do not require things of the world to spread light and joy. There is no rationale to covet what others have or remain insecure from our inferior thoughts. We do not hinder our intended progress. We were equipped long ago and use exactly what we have to make an impact.

Anger

WHEN WE EXHIBIT ANGER, we move within a volatile emotion. It can lead to dangerous choices and broken situations which are often difficult to remedy. Reasons for ensuing anger have seemingly narrow origins but can quickly spread into other realms.

A common culprit is at the helm of this emotion: expectations. We may have experienced disappointments; overlooked promises; less-than-ideal outcomes; or things we perceived but did not receive. Through these situations, anger develops when assumptions do not come to pass. And often, the level of anger exhibited is dictated by how deserving we felt.

Anger frequently begins as hurt. With increased time—contemplating, reliving, or rethinking—it surfaces. Depending on the state of our souls and spirits, it may be an instant explosion based on the feeling of complete let-down. It can become an adopted reaction if it has been a familiar display by others around us.

When someone is considered to have an angry personality, it is due to reactions. Over time, our habitual outbursts can develop into part of our character and can be difficult to overcome. But God moves in what seems to be the impossible. As we read in Exodus, if we trust him—and stop attempting to take control—God will fight for us.

Justification and blame often accompany anger. This is due to guilt of overreactions and preference of a more wholesome self-view. For true vision into the circumstance, we seek the help of the Holy Spirit. The more we justify our right for anger, the more we remain a prisoner to this deceiving emotion. Our bodies and minds react negatively. We often usher stress and disease into our lives due to the weight of turbulent responses.

When we exhibit anger, we exercise an extreme reaction that can metaphorically be viewed as a fire. Tempers flare and create flames that rise higher and into greater intensity. Those nearby will not venture near the blaze out of fear of injury. Our fires can quickly ignite everything around us. When they finally subside, we are left standing in a pile of destruction and ash. Sometimes we even grow angry at ourselves for dragging others into the chaotic environment. Yet we struggle to stop acting enraged.

Perhaps we have grown irritated toward the promises of God, and feel infuriated that he failed to grant a need. Or maybe we interpreted his Word with individual intentions and assumed a conclusion. When this does not come to pass, there is a tendency to blame the One we feel should have been our Source. Misguided emotions will attempt to place fault. But deep in our spirits, we know the truth. God loves us and does not bring us harm. Or grant less than optimal results.

God desires that we seek him and count on his wisdom and strength. He guides us away from destructive paths. Isaiah 54 says, "No weapon forged against you will prevail" (v. 17). We must remember that our battles are not against flesh and blood in this world. Often, we gauge anger by our surroundings and immediate views instead of the actual culprits—spiritual entities. In turn, our emotions are displaced and affect those close by.

With discipline, we begin to see others in the light that God intended, even if they are not the most loving or kind. He will rescue us from temptation to display disapproval in an angry manner. God will deliver us from that form of evil and usher us into a realm that births gentleness and kindness. "I will give them an undivided heart and put a new spirit in them; I will remove from them their heart of stone and give them a heart of flesh" (Ezek 11:19).

Remember that gentleness is anchored with great power. "A hot-tempered person stirs up conflict, but the one who is patient calms a quarrel" (Prov 15:18). God will lead us, but we must be willing and seek him.

Our Father also wants to redeem us. Even when we have severely damaged situations or relationships, it is never too late. The death and resurrection of Jesus was God's plan for our redemption. The power of the cross was initiated long ago but is still perfect in its unmatched reliability. The power pertains to *all* situations including fiery tempers, intense encounters, and ruptured relationships.

"To bestow on them a crown of beauty instead of ashes, the oil of joy instead of mourning, and a garment of praise instead of a spirit of despair. They will be called oaks of righteousness, a planting of the Lord for the display of his splendor" (Isa 61:3). Our Father desires that we experience his grace and redemption where we have fallen short. We praise him for replacing our anger and despair with joy. We emerge more in his likeness. A reminder that we are his beloved children.

Doubt

We have discussed the formation of emotions from thoughts and circumstances. And that actions lead to specific characteristics. We examined fruits of the Spirit that encompass our character when allowing God to lead. Our positive traits stem from these fruits. Negative emotions are often birthed when following the path of the enemy. "Do not be misled: 'Bad company corrupts good character" (1 Cor 15:33).

We know that God created us. He gave us free will. His truths lead and grant strength. But the enemy delivers doubt into our lives even with the acceptance of our creation in God's image. We acknowledge that our path is dependent on choices. And whether we maintain a relationship—surrendered and obedient to God.

Our emotions are powerful and can lead to grueling situations and negative reactions. They bring suffering and steer us in the wrong direction. These steps may be camouflaged by what appears to be authentic. Often, we follow feelings and permit them to guide decisions, while convincing ourselves we are on the correct path. Until the realization sets in that we have been deceived.

We agonize when things come crashing down and often blame ourselves. Disdain for our impressions and decisions grows, or for misleading thoughts from others that we trusted. Negative emotions increase toward the situation and those involved.

These circumstances can cause a view of self that saddens our Father, because we are his beloved. Instead of walking in the likeness of God, we become easily exhausted and feel broken. We begin to doubt our own abilities and choices.

God did not expect us to operate in control and assume answers. He has a supreme perspective of every scope of our lives and intends to accompany us. But too often we undertake every aspect of our journey alone.

When things go poorly, it promotes doubt. It may even be directed at God, because we feel he failed to reveal his ability when we anticipated. But he is never absent. Only quiet, due to his perfect timing in all things.

Our doubt is frequently in self. We possess the mindset that we are unable to bring accomplishments to completion. In addition, our doubt can be focused on situations and people. We lose faith in humanity and question the authenticity of our relationships. However, we cannot have an expectation of fulfillment by the world. This was never intended. Only God is our Source. "And my God will meet all your needs according to the riches of his glory in Christ Jesus" (Phil 4:19).

Just as we have discussed the names of God, we recognize that he delivers many benefits. Psalm 103 shows that God is: a forgiver, healer, compassionate, loving, patient, gentle, and full of grace and mercy. He delivers justice and is the redeemer from eternal death. He is a good Father.

Through the choice to invite God into our hearts, our spirits are reborn. We have a home with God for eternity. He renews our souls and ushers in the fruits of the Spirit: love, joy, peace, patience, kindness, goodness, gentleness, faithfulness, and self-control. God also restores our bodies when we hope for healing. We recognize him as our power and strength.

When we focus on these truths, we begin to overcome doubt. Our uncertainty and hesitations are replaced with hope and faith. But we must develop a genuine and solid foundation before building, or we crumble under the weight of counterfeit framework. Especially if we are not prepared or move quickly without guidance.

Our thoughts and emotions appear real but place us in daily battles. We feel steadfast when things are satisfactory but struggle with challenges. This is demonstration of a foundational concept. If not authentic, we waiver. God's Word—with its reliability— is a compass for our everyday survival. When we sustain an accurate focus, the fruits of his Spirit shine even in difficult times. They create in us a more Christ-like character.

Considering a worldly perspective, the necessity for strong footing is imperative. We do not build houses on unlevel ground without securing the site. Neither do we succeed when we maneuver a journey without relying on God's strength and his promises.

Once we understand this concept, it becomes our basis—and guidance—when our lives are turned upside down. We believe a strong framework—purposefully placed—doubles as protection. It shields and keeps us from harm. Distractions will arise to tempt and lead us into the wilderness. But God recognizes these interruptions and shepherds us while granting clarity. He will lead us from doubt as we maintain a foundation in him.

Conclusion

A POWERFUL CONCLUSION TO this journey of emergence is a reminder that the cross allowed more freedom than we deserve and displayed more love than we could ever imagine. It delivered justice for sins that should have been ours to pay. An amazing and unsurpassed grace and a mercy that endures forever. Jesus does not *represent* these examples. He *is* the blueprint. His actions invite an unmistakable view of love. And we witness the extent of how much he cares with wisdom the Bible shares.

When we feel deeply and it causes pain, he heals. If we misstep because we assume accuracy, he redeems. When we make poor choices, he forgives. If our character has been damaged, the Holy Spirit guides us to renewal through his fruits.

In continuing the steps of this journey, we magnify the gifts of mercy and grace. Both are freely given without expectation. God's gestures display these virtues. It is important to realize their enormity, and how they are relevant to emergence.

Grace is a gift we receive from God daily. His grace is always enough. "My grace is sufficient for you, for my power is made perfect in weakness" (2 Cor 12:9). God shows us that he provides abundantly. We only need to embrace him. Our Father's continuous gesture of grace is freely given—and shows favor—although we are underserving. Nothing we do will make us worthy of the fullness of God's grace. It is reflected by his deep love and because of his desire for relationship. Not by our attempts to earn it.

Mercy is the means of granting escape when punishment should have been received. It is represented by God giving us a pass, even though we are underserving. Mercy is shown by our Father, not just once, but over again each day. "The steadfast love of the Lord never ceases; his mercies never come to an end; they are new every morning, great is your faithfulness" (Lam 3:22–23).

By these two amazing gifts, God sincerely shows the depths of his love. Nothing to be earned, only freely given. One alone would be beyond our comprehension. But together, they render an overwhelming sense of relief and appreciation. The journey of emergence is not easy, but we must remember that it is intertwined daily with the actions of God. It brings comfort to realize this has been ordained.

Grace and mercy propel us forward. They put new wind in our sails when we awaken and face another day. They give us the fuel we need to continue our path on God's course. Thanks to our Father's plan—with love and power—we are encompassed by his faithfulness daily. Not only does he continuously show us unmerited favor, but he designed an escape. His amazing grace and mercy that lives forever.

www.ingramcontent.com/pod-product-compliance
Lightning Source LLC
LaVergne TN
LVHW020648100826
845148LV00012B/2387

* 9 7 8 1 6 6 6 7 1 2 3 1 5 *